American Men of Letters.

EDITED BY

CHARLES DUDLEY WARNER.

Painted by S.F.B.Morse.   A.W. Elson & Co. Boston.

N. Webster

American Men of Letters.

NOAH WEBSTER.

BY

HORACE E. SCUDDER.

BOSTON:
HOUGHTON, MIFFLIN AND COMPANY.
NEW YORK: 11 EAST SEVENTEENTH STREET.
The Riverside Press, Cambridge.
1892.

The Riverside Press, Cambridge, Mass , U. S. A.

Electrotyped and Printed by H. O. Houghton & Company

CONTENTS.

CHAPTER VIII.

Acknowledgment is due to Mr. Gordon L. Ford, of Brooklyn, N. Y., for the valuable assistance which he has rendered by permitting the author to make use of his admirable collection of printed and manuscript material relating to Noah Webster.

NOAH WEBSTER.

CHAPTER I.

EARLY LIFE.

THE village of West Hartford lies about three miles from the centre of Hartford and is mainly grouped about two cross-roads, one leading from the city west to Farmington, the other, the village street, following the line of the Connecticut River and rambling from Bloomfield, the next village north, to Newington and New Britain on the south. The changes in the place for the last hundred and fifty years have not been great; the Farmington road, to be sure, as it leaves Hartford, keeps a city character and shows trim villas at intervals nearly all the way to the village, but the village has not moved to meet the city, and its houses and one or two churches and post-office have admitted new-comers so slowly that the general air of the place can scarcely be different from what it was in 1758, when Noah Webster was born there, October 16. The house in which he was born is still standing, about a mile from the corners, on the road leading south; it is upon a broad table-land, and the wide fields which lie below it, stretching away to Talcott Mountain, where the western view ends, are the fields which Webster's father planted.

The ancestral stock was substantial. Noah Webster remembered the funeral of his grandfather Daniel, and Daniel was five years old when his grandfather died, who was one of the first settlers in Hartford and Governor of Connecticut. The family had lived thus in this district for five generations, as farmers, long lived and good citizens. The place where Webster was born was sold by his father in 1790 to the family whose representatives now live there; it covered eighty acres then, but has been broken in upon from time to time. The senior Webster sold it because he was poor. He lived his life of ninety-one years in a Connecticut village, leaving it only when he led

a company for one campaign in the Revolutionary War. His square, upright tomb-
stone stands in the village graveyard, and
commemorates the stocky virtues of integrity and piety. He was Deacon Webster
and Squire Webster, and reached thus the
highest offices in state and church which a
little New England village could offer.

Upon the senior Webster's stone is the
name of his wife Mercy, who is comprehen-
sively disposed of as "his consort, equally
respected for her piety and virtues." She
was a descendant of William Bradford, the
Plymouth governor, and thus the two lives
which met in Noah Webster were Pilgrim
and Puritan, without, it appears, any quar-
tering from other sources. All the Websters were a sturdy race. Noah Webster,
senior, died in his ninety-second year; Noah
the son in his eighty-fifth; his two brothers
lived for eighty years or more, and his two
sisters for seventy. Out of the scanty memoranda of the family genealogy little more
is to be gleaned, but it is enough for our
purpose to know that the man, whose fortunes we are to follow, inherited the Puritan mind and the New England constitution.

He had, what every New England family wished to give a boy who had any quickness of intellect, the education that was at the door. He worked on his father's farm and went to the village school where rarely a book was used except a spelling-book, a psalter, a Testament or a Bible. When he was fourteen years old he had shown that he was of the college kind, and studying for two years with Dr. Perkins, the village minister, and in the Hopkins Grammar School at Hartford, he entered Yale College in 1774. There were about a hundred and fifty students in New Haven at that time, with a faculty consisting of a Professor of Divinity, who performed the duties of President, a Professor of Mathematics and Natural Philosophy, and three tutors. Joel Barlow was a classmate, and so were Oliver Wolcott, Zephaniah Smith, Ashur Miller, and others who occupied high judicial positions afterward in the young republic. In Dr. Stiles's Diary there is an entry June 14, 1778, Webster's senior year. " The students disputed forensically this day a twofold question ; whether the destruction of the Alexandrian Library and the ignorance of the Middle Ages, caused by the inundation of the Goths and Vandals, were events unfortunate to literature. They disputed inimitably well, particularly Barlow, Swift, and Webster."

There is something peculiarly felicitous in this grave record. It was a rotund kind of learning which was cherished by Dr. Stiles and similar guardians of the old traditions of scholarship, and in the absence of much commerce with their intellectual peers beyond the limits of the colonies, each college made believe very hard that its students were scholars, and its scholastic life the counterpart of historic universities. But it is easy to believe that the fate of the Alexandrián Library and the performances of the notorious Goths and Vandals, those favorite and dimly understood barbarians, had no such power in determining the education of the young Yale student as had the events of the war then going on. Webster had entered college in the fall of 1774; in the spring of 1775, while he was still a Freshman, he had his little initiation into Revolutionary society. General Washington was on his way to Cambridge, to take

command of the American army, and with
him was General Charles Lee. They passed
through New Haven, and Webster has left
a little sketch of the scene.

" These gentlemen lodged in New Haven,
at the house of the late Isaac Beers, and in
the morning they were invited to see a military company of students of Yale College
perform their manual exercises. They expressed their surprise and gratification at
the precision with which the students performed the customary exercises then in use.
This company then escorted the generals as
far as Neck Bridge, and this was the first
instance of that honor conferred on General
Washington in New England. It fell to
my humble lot to lead this company with
music."

The last sentence is a faint hint at an
amusing and pardonable little vanity of
Webster's, who, as the reader will discover
later, liked to think that he had a hand in
pretty much every important measure in
the political and literary history of the
country in those early days, and remembered that when the great Washington appeared, Webster was ready with the prelu-

sive fife. The three years which followed
were years of excitement and distraction.
In the summer of 1777 the college life at New
Haven was broken up, and the classes were
disposed in various towns, the Junior class,
in which Webster belonged, being stationed
at Glastonbury and placed under the charge
of Tutor Buckminster. This was the time
when all New England, especially the southern part, was thrown into a ferment by Burgoyne's movements, and men were hurried
into the field to meet this army coming
down from the north. Webster's father
was captain in the alarm list, and Webster
shouldered his musket as a private in his
father's company. The episode was probably in the summer vacation, and put a stop
to his work on the farm rather than to his
studies in college. Burgoyne's defeat re-
leased the young volunteer, but an education which was divided between the camp
and the cloister was pretty sure to be fruit-
ful in something beside scholastic learning.
A college, scattered as if by the enemy's
bombs into country villages, was likely to
think with all the eagerness of youth upon
questions of political ethics, and of the broad

grounds of human freedom. There are two
words often used in the ephemeral literature of that day, — *slave, free,* — words used
somewhat recklessly at times, but marking
the general current of men's thoughts.

Webster, in one of his reminiscences, re-
calls the wretched condition of affairs when
he was in college : "So impoverished was
the country at one time," he writes, "that
the steward of the college could not supply
the necessary provisions of the table, and
the students were compelled to return to
spend several months at home. At one
time goods were so scarce that the farmers
cut corn-stalks and crushed them in cider-
mills, and then boiled the juice down to a
syrup as a substitute for sugar." The years
which followed his graduation were, if anything, still more discouraging. When he
went home, after Commencement, his father
gave him an eight-dollar bill of the Continental currency, worth then about fifty cents
on the dollar, and left him to his own resources. His plan was to study law, but his
first business was to maintain himself, and
he took up school-teaching, spending the
winter of 1778 in Glastonbury, where he

had gone with his class the year before. In the summer of 1779 he returned to Hartford and taught there, living in the family of Mr., afterward Chief Justice, Oliver Ellsworth, and picking up a little law. In the hard winter of 1780 he taught in his native village, and in the next summer he lived with and assisted Jedediah Strong, register of deeds in Litchfield, where he read law, and then was admitted to the bar in Hartford.

There was, however, no business. People were too poor to go to law, and the whole country was depressed by its condition. The struggle for independence had not been a short, sharp one, marked by an intense flame of enthusiasm; the end was reached less by heroic endeavor than by heroic patience and the wisdom of a few. The depths of ignominy into which Continental currency had sunk measured the hopelessness with which those who lived by wits rather than by manual labor surveyed the field. So, relinquishing the law, Webster resumed teaching, this time in Sharon. An advertisement gives notice of what he expected to do in his school : —

" On the first of May will be opened, at Sharon in Connecticut, a school, in which children may be instructed, not only in the common arts of reading, writing, and arithmetic, but in any branch of academical literature. The little regard that is paid to the literary improvement of females, even among people of rank and fortune, and the general inattention to the grammatical purity and elegance of our native language, are faults in the education of youth that more gentlemen have taken pains to censure than correct. Any young gentlemen and ladies, who wish to acquaint themselves with the English language, geography, vocal music, &c., may be waited on at particular hours for that purpose. The price of board and tuition will be from six to nine shillings lawful money per week, according to the age and studies of the scholar; no pains will be spared to render the school useful.   Noah Webster.

" Sharon, *April* 16, 1782.

" N. B. The subscriber has a large convenient store in Sharon fit for storing articles of any kind, where they may be secured at a moderate expense."

One would like to know if R—— P——
was one of the young ladies upon whom he
waited at some particular hour, for tradition tells of the young teacher, with a commanding figure and erect carriage, very
careful in dress and precise in speech, spar-
ing no pains not only to render the school
useful but himself agreeable to this young
lady, who found, however, a stronger attrac-
tion in a soldier lover, soldiers having then,
as later, a singular advantage in such rival-
ries. This precise-speaking young school-
master was ready enough for a frolic, as may
be guessed from two consecutive entries in
his brief diary, a little later: —

"*Feb.* 18, 1784. At evening rode to
Wethersfield [from Hartford, where he was
then living] with the ladies, who reminded
us of the mile-stones and bridges." [Does
any one now need to be told why?]

"*Feb.* 19, P. M. Rode to East Wind-
sor; had a clergyman with us, who sang an
excellent song. Mile-stones and bridges almost totally neglected."

The demure mouth with which this last
sentence is spoken must have had a curl at
the corner occasionally. While living at

Sharon he took the opportunity to study French with a M. Tetard, a French Protestant minister living in New Rochelle.

From the scanty records which remain I have traced thus far Webster's early life and education, but it is fair to find in his subsequent career traces of the influence which New England surroundings cast about every New England boy. The simplicity of life which characterized a province so uniform in its character was especially evident in the Connecticut Valley. Here, longer than in the cities and on the sea-board, native English and Puritan stock retained the form and power which an unbroken succession in blood and a freedom from external pressure had made possible. The families known by Webster in his boyhood, among whom he lived, and whose lives passed into his character, were a part of the great migration which founded a new England between 1630 and 1640, and from a basis of English law and custom, modified by theocratic doctrines, and partially shaped by a struggle with the wilderness, built a state which was to be one of the great forces in

American history. The agricultural life, which was more productive in the valley of the Connecticut than elsewhere, determined largely the social life of the colony, made Connecticut the most serenely democratic of the New England States, emphasized the individual worth, and allowed free play in self-government. The church held its own for a longer period than in Massachusetts; the inevitable surrender of the ecclesiastical power of the Congregationalists was deferred until a much later date; and to-day it is in Hartford that one will find most distinctly the lines of colonial Congregationalism.

The life of the household in a Connecticut village in the middle of the eighteenth century was very self-centred. Remote from towns, — for Hartford was only a village then, — the demands of farming life determined the round of days. Every one from childhood fell of necessity into his or her place as one of the workers, out doors and in, and the simplicity of the social organization made the farmer a mechanic as well. There was the blacksmith's shop, where a rudely trained skill supplied the more special needs; but the farmer himself not only used his tools, but mended and to some extent made them; he was carpenter also, and shoemaker, and, in general, necessity had taught his hands to shape and his fingers to be dexterous. The boy made his own traps and small tools and carts, and early learned that handiness and adaptability without which he would be likely to go through life in a destitute condition. There is to be found still, especially in the back country, a curious survival of this old economy in the hired man, who shines in literature in the person of Mr. Jacob Abbott's Jonas, the embodiment of practical wisdom, learned not so much from books as from the daily school of farm and shop life. The hired man of that time was the occasional unattached member of society, or one who was forced out of the family hive by the excess of hands and the deficiency of land. Commonly the family itself supplied the necessary laborers, and these all in their youth, no matter what intellectual promise they might give, were, as a matter of course, parts of the regular farm company.

The jack-of-all-trades character of the

farmer and the absence of a force of arti-
sans and special craftsmen easily compelled
a state of mutual dependence. If a house
or a barn were to be built, the neighborhood was called in at the critical moment
to raise the frame; and the farmer who
asked the help made his acknowledgment
not only by serving when his neighbor
needed him, but by acting as host to the
company, and making the raising a time of
good cheer and hilarity. Harvest also gave
opportunity for mutual help and neighborly
charity, so that much of the social life of
the day grew naturally out of the common
work and occupation of the community.
In-doors it was the same, and quilting bees
and huskings and spinning bees made work
and play shade into each other. A community where every one worked and each
might be needed by his neighbor would
scarcely suffer very marked distinctions of
rank; and in the lighter social life, which
made no pretense of work, the sleighing
parties and athletic sports, the suppers and
dances which followed the bees, an equality
of condition was assumed, very favorable to
self-respect and independence of judgment.

It is to be noticed that the substitution of alphabetical order in college classes for a rank based upon social distinction occurred earlier at Yale than at Harvard, and it is not unlikely that the more democratic life of Connecticut had something to do with it.

Distinctions, however, there were, but they were laid chiefly in reasons which all were willing to accept. The magistrate and the clergyman, though familiar associates of the plainer people, were conceded a deference which superior education, and not superior birth, compelled, and without question the road to eminence was held to lie through education. No one dreamed of securing the special honor of the community except by this means, and in every family a boy who showed intellectual promise was encouraged to hope for a college education. His college education was in most cases expected to result in an entrance to the clerical profession, but the law had by this time begun to have a more distinct claim upon attention, and the medical profession had always demanded those who could show a positive predilection for it.[1]

[1] An examination of the Yale catalogue shows that,

The doctor, however, did not learn his science under any organized educational system, but by personal association and study with an older practitioner, a system which naturally lessened the likelihood of persons drifting into the profession upon slight grounds of preference. The self-contained life of the community, indeed, made people somewhat indifferent to a highly educated medical profession, and increased also the confidence with which any one might assume to observe and discuss facts connected with the art and science of healing. In every household there was traditional learning which served for ordinary purposes, and the housewife knew and used herbs with something of the practical wisdom which she applied to her cooking. In every community there was likely to be one woman or more to whom the rest turned in emergencies, and a rude practice was kept

with some fluctuations, the proportion of clerical alumni to the whole number of graduates fell off pretty surely during the middle of the century. In the decades marked by Webster's graduation, the proportion was roughly as follows: in 1748, nearly one half the class entered the ministry; in 1758, nearly one third; in 1768 one fourth; in 1778, one tenth.

2

up which cannot be called quackery, for it was entirely unpretentious. Something also was due to the knowledge derived from the Indians, whose closeness to nature was supposed to give them excellent opportunities for wresting secrets from simples. This respect for the Indian school survives still, and affords a support to the queer practitioners who call themselves Indian Doctors. It was never strange, therefore, when a man who had received a liberal education turned his attention to questions which nowadays a layman would scarcely venture to discuss. He was not regarded as an amateur, but as occupying himself with a legitimate part of his business.

Even more surely was the educated man a lawyer. There was always a good deal of litigation going on in Connecticut, but the legal profession scarcely existed as a distinct body until Webster himself came upon the stage. Plaintiff and defendant addressed the court if they desired, and in the loose practice of the day there were no intricate and technical processes which debarred any intelligent man from taking part in a cause. Substantial justice was done, and every citi-

zen took part in legal affairs with confidence
that he only needed perseverance and a fair
cause to achieve success. Above all, the
constant and familiar participation in public concerns was a school for the citizen, in
which he learned thoroughly the art of legislation, and acquired a readiness in government which stood him in good stead when
the scope of governmental power was en-
larged. The New England town was always the centre of political life, and each
member of the town learned early his in-
alienable right to a participation in all the
benefits which the community could confer.
In town-meeting he learned to vote and to
be voted for; a gradation of offices from
fence-viewer or hog-reeve to selectman gave
training in administration to all who had
any capacity for organization or leadership;
the discussion of town affairs sharpened the
wits, and, better still, educated the towns-
man in a distinct recognition of his political relations; he learned to think politically,
and as the Revolution drew near, the petty
interests of the local community widened
into larger questions of state when the towns
themselves found that they were parts of a

larger body corporate. Then the principle of representation was constantly delocalizing the town, and bringing into the arena subjects which reminded men of their relationship to the state and the crown. Men who had grown up under the discussion of questions which involved great historic processes were not likely, when the occasion came, to hold back from writing or speaking on great national themes, merely because they were not publicists by profession.

The military system, which formed so important a part of the New Englander's education, added to the picturesqueness of his life and to the notion of solidarity. The experience with Indian and Frenchman, as has often been shown, had made the unostentatious farmer-soldiers of New England a formidable and resolute body when the day of the Revolution came. Before that day the train-bands of the towns were the color and music of the otherwise monotonous life. Four times a year came muster with its drill, its competitive shooting, its feasting, its sports, and its exercise of self-government in the election of officers. This

visible expression of the power of the community generated a self-confidence and a
spirit of generous comradery in the mind
of the young soldier ; the courage which it
gave, the habit of standing upright in any
presence, the belief that back of the voice
lay the strong arm, were parts of the education of such men as Webster.

Of the more specific literary education I
have already spoken. Webster's training
as a scholar was that of other Americans of
his day, neither better nor worse ; and indeed there was not much to choose between
the chances of town and country. So late
as 1813 Mr. George Ticknor, in his reminiscences, relates his difficulties in undertaking the study of German in Boston : " At
Jamaica Plains there was a Dr. Brosius, a
native of Strasburg, who gave instruction
in mathematics. He was willing to do what
he could for me in German, but he warned
me that his pronunciation was very bad, as
was that of all Alsace, which had become a
part of France. Nor was it possible to get
books. I borrowed a Meidinger's grammar,
French and German, from my friend Mr.
Everett, and sent to New Hampshire, where

I knew there was a German dictionary, and procured it. I also obtained a copy of Goethe's ' Werther' in German (through Mr. William S. Shaw's connivance) from amongst Mr. J. Q. Adams's books, deposited by him, on going to Europe, in the Athenæum, under Mr. Shaw's care, but without giving him permission to lend them." [1] Mr. Hillard, in commenting on this, says well that " there are now, doubtless, more facilities in New England for the study of Arabic or Persian than there were then for the study of German." But it was not yet even 1813 in Hartford and its neighborhood, and in the middle of the eighteenth century the literary resources were meagre in the extreme. Learning was not concentrated in the towns, but the access to books there was easier. The country minister, who was the scholar, literary man, and school-master, fell back largely upon the Greek and Latin classics, and upon the few books of the day which he could get in his rare journeys to Boston. In Boston itself there were book-stores, and John Mein, afterward a royalist

[1] *Life, Letters, and Journals of George Ticknor,* i. 11, 12.

refugee, kept a circulating library in 1765 at what was known as the London bookstore. It numbered some twelve hundred volumes, and boasted a printed catalogue. It gives some indication of the condition of the book business in Boston that he advertised, about ten years before the outbreak of the war, a stock of above ten thousand volumes. If Dr. Perkins, Noah Webster's school-master, went to New Haven to draw books from the college library, he found there in 1765 " a good library, consisting of about four thousand volumes, well furnished with ancient authors, such as the Fathers, Historians, and Classics; many modern valuable books of divinity, history, philosophy, and mathematics ; but not many authors who have wrote within these thirty years." [1]

We are more concerned to know the kind of reading which was at Webster's command when a boy outside of his school hours. That the severer literature dominated seems evident from the recourse which he has to it in his writings when he wishes illustrations; for, like others of his day, the

[1] *President Clap's Annals,* under date of 1765.

classic authors, especially of Rome, were
quoted with a sense of their being final
authority.   The newspaper in Webster's
youth had scarcely yet asserted itself very
forcibly.   The few centres of population
had journals, which did not travel very far
beyond the place of publication.   The Connecticut " Courant," a weekly newspaper,
was started in Hartford in 1764, and was
of the better class, poorly printed, but serving as a medium for communications from
its readers; the leading article was anticipated by the letter to the editor or printer,
and with the exception of a scanty abstract of news the " Courant " may be said
to have been edited by its subscribers, — a
policy which made such papers very good
reflections of the feeling of the community.
Older and better established than the newspaper was the almanac, which throve in New
England and performed a familiar service in
every household.   Mr. Ames or Mr. Lord,
and their fellows, addressed readers in the
jaunty, unconventional style which was regarded as appropriate to a class of literature which was neither fish, flesh, nor fowl,
and after their preliminary talk and their

monthly calendar, with its wonderful comments, gave the page or two that remained
to anecdotes, poetry, and miscellaneous literature. The calendar was headed by verse,
which was taken usually from English authors of the time, and sometimes was treated
serially. Thus in one almanac the poem of
" Porsenna in pursuit of the Kingdom of
Felicity" trails along the head of the twelve
months, and at the end is announced to be
continued next year; next year it starts on
its journey again, and overflows upon one of
the extra pages, but still is unfinished; a
third year it makes a desperate effort to come
to an end, but the editor is obliged to an-
nounce, " Conclusion omitted this year for
want of room;" and only when a fourth
year has come is he able to get rid of this
continued poem. Think of the impatience
of readers who had to wait from year to
year for four years before they could finish
reading this work of art! As the years
of the war drew near, the contents of these
little books took on a more martial character, and the poetical *feuilleton* gave place
to a military chronicle.

Jejune enough do these hints seem to

make the life in which Webster grew up:
but if it was poverty-stricken as compared
with the abundant resources of our own
day, — if the Hartford of 1765 is to be contrasted with that of 1881, to the manifest
disadvantage of the former, — one would
wish to remember that in the very sterility
of that life there was a certain iron which
entered into the constitution of the people
who lived it. If there were not the leisure
and culture of the present day, neither were
there the mental indolence and dissipation.
Ames's Almanac was a joyless sort of light
literature, but at least it did not reduce intellectual recreation to a mere frivolous in-
dulgence of the mental faculties. A fine
picture could be drawn of Webster on the
one side, extracting what juice he could
from the chippy leaves of the almanac and
"Courant," and of a youth of this year,
entering a public library with his card, and
having the range of a hundred thousand
volumes; but the real comparison is to be
made between the results in character and
production. We are painfully familiar with
the lists of books which constitute the reading of the average boy of to-day, and know

perfectly well that they are very often nar-
cotic and stimulant. The reading which
was had with such difficulty in the middle
of the eighteenth century may sometimes
have acted as a sedative, but it was by
reason of quality and scarcity more generally brave food; in the mind of the reader
there was an immense respect for literature
which induced a genuine hunger for books,
and the individuality of one who had intellectual tastes was not impaired, as so often
happens now, but fortified and enriched.

The farm, the social round, the school,
the college, the out-door sports, the in-door
books and papers, were all parts of the circumstance which affected the life of the
youth, but no picture of the time would
be complete which omitted the influence
upon him of the church. He would grow
up with the impression that the meeting-
house was the principal building in town,
the minister the principal person, and Sunday the principal day. A curious illustration of the strong hold which the religious
observance of Sunday had upon the colo-
nists then is in the construction of what
were known as Sabbath-Day Houses, which

I think were peculiar to Connecticut. At
any rate, there is so good a description of
them by a son-in-law of Webster's that I
give it here: —

" These houses were from twenty to
twenty-five feet in length, and from ten
to twelve feet in breadth, and one story
high, with a chimney in the middle, divid-
ing the whole space into two rooms, with a
partition between them, for the accommo-
dation of two families, who united in building the house. The furniture consisted of
a few chairs, a table, plates and dishes,
some iron utensil, it may be, for warming
food which had been cooked. Besides the
Bible, there was sometimes a book on ex-
perimental religion, like Baxter's 'Saints'
Rest,' or Allein's 'Alarm.' On the morning of the Sabbath the mother of the family,
with provident care, put up her store of
comforts for the dinner, substantial or slight
fare as most convenient, a bottle of cider
almost of course. The family then set off
from their home in a large two-horse sleigh,
or on saddles and pillions. They stopped
at the Sabbath-day house, kindled a blaz-
ing fire, and then went forth to shiver in

the cold during the morning services. At noon they hurried back to their warm room. After they had taken their meal, and by turns drunk from the pewter mug, thanks were returned. Then the sermon came under review, from the notes taken by the father of the family, or a chapter was read from the Bible, or a paragraph from some favorite author, the service concluding with prayer or singing. After again visiting the sanctuary, the family would return to the Sabbath-day house, if the cold was severe, before they sought their home. The fire was then extinguished, the door was locked, and the house remained undisturbed during the week. In time the custom of repairing to these houses changed; the houses themselves became dilapidated, or furnished a refuge for the poor. They were better suited to those times, when so much was thought of private family religion, than they would be to ours, when religion has become more of a public and social concern. The last Sabbath-day house which I remember stood on the land owned by the first minister. It was occupied by John King, a Hessian deserter from the British army. It

was owned by one of the Nortons. The
present writer can recollect as many as half
a dozen of these houses." [1]

The legislation thrown about the Sabbath was in confirmation of the public opinion regarding its sanctity. The harsher
aspects of this observance have been sufficiently dwelt upon in our histories ; the effect upon character has been less considered,
but the elevation of one day out of the tyranny of work, the resolute facing of eternal
mysteries, and the withdrawal into a half-
brooding, half-active state of mind must
have had a powerful effect upon the imag-
ination and conscience. The meeting-house
was no holy building, but the Sabbath day
was a holy day, and was the most comprehensive symbol of the Puritan faith. It
was what the altar is in the Catholic Church,
the holy of holies, about which the whole
movement of religious worship gathered.
Whatever disturbed the profound stillness
of the day was seized upon by the law as
sacrilegious ; and never, perhaps, has there
been a religion which succeeded so com-

1 *History of Durham, Connecticut.* By William Chauncey Fowler, LL. D., pp. 97, 98.

pletely in investing time with the sacred-
ness which elsewhere had been appropriated
by place. Even the approach to the Sabbath was guarded, and the custom of the
observance of Saturday evening appears to
have been derived from the backward influence of the day, as the release upon Sunday
evening appears to have been a concession
to the flesh, which would otherwise have
rebelled. Dr. Bushnell, in his "Age of
Homespun," tells of his own experience in
boyhood, when he was refused a load of apples, which he had gone to buy on Saturday
afternoon, because the farmer, on consulting
the sun, decided that he could not measure
out the fruit before the strict Sabbath began.

The minister again represented to the
young New Englander the highest expression of human attainment. He was right-
eous and he was learned. Learning he had
in a severe and lofty form, and though there
was little in his outward dress to mark him
as a priest of God, he was isolated from the
community by his authority and profession,
so that he answered rather to one's conception of a prophet. Before him were brought

offenders against Sabbath decorum, and the minister's study was to the boy the most awful room into which he could enter. This association of learning with piety served to heighten still further the respect with which learning was regarded, and to separate the young student almost by a special laying on of hands. The minister also usually had his glebe, and held a common interest with the farmers of the neighborhood, — a humanizing relation which had much to do in preserving the real respect in which he was held. The positive influence of religion upon life, by being identified with the highest intellectualism and the most eminent persons, had thus both its strength and weakness. There was wanting the large and comprehensive spirit of an historic church ; there was the peril of a too abstract regard for religion ; but on the other hand there was a very strong stimulus to individualism. No one with any force of character could grow up under these influences without being vigorously affected by them.

CHAPTER II.

THE GRAMMATICAL INSTITUTE.

"IN the year 1782, while the American army was lying on the bank of the Hudson, I kept a classical school in Goshen, Orange County, State of New York. I there compiled two small elementary books for teaching the English language. The country was then impoverished, intercourse with Great Britain was interrupted, school-books were scarce and hardly attainable, and there was no certain prospect of peace."

These words have doubtless a familiar sound to the reader. They form the phrases which Webster never wearied of repeating, and whenever he had occasion to refer to the beginning of his literary career he fell naturally into this paragraph. It became a formula for the expression of a fact which was embedded in his mind as a stone marking a point of departure. There is a consciousness in it of the beginning of a great

3

enterprise, and certainly, when one considers the immense stream which has flowed from this little rill, he may seriously stand and gaze at the young school-master and his two small elementary books. The modesty of the statement agrees with the size of the books, but not with the expansiveness of the composite title. The work projected by Webster was "A Grammatical Institute of the English Language, comprising an Easy, Concise, and Systematic Method of Education, designed for the Use of English Schools in America." The "Institute" was to be in three parts, which were, in brief, a speller, a grammar, and a reader. The formal and dignified title of the work was the tribute which Webster paid to old-fashioned scholarship; and it is curious to see the evolution by which it finally became the well-known "Elementary." One or two ideas were working their way out in Webster's mind. In the first place he did not like the book generally in use, "Dilworth's New Guide to the English Tongue;" then he saw with more or less clearness that, in the separation from England that was fast taking place, the people in America must necessarily have their own school-books, and his mind ran forward even to a belief in a distinct and separate literature and a considerable difference in language. Yet at this time I am not sure that he appreciated the pregnant truth, so familiar to us now, of a vital connection between popular education and popular sovereignty. He began to see it, and was influenced by it; but his work was mightier than he then knew, for he had not been educated in a free republic.

How simple and slight a change in methods of text-books marks the introduction of Webster's spelling-book, from which millions of Americans have learned to spell the names on a ballot! Lay Dilworth and a first Webster side by side: the likeness and the difference of the two are apparent. It is clear that Dilworth served as a model, and that Webster's book started simply as an improvement upon the English original. Even in externals there is a similarity. The early editions of Webster had a dim, hacked-out engraving on wood of Noah Webster, Jr., Esq., to correspond with the scarcely more refined portrait of Tho. Dil-

worth which prefaces the "New Guide."
Both books have long lists of words, pro-
ceeding from the simplest combination to
words of five syllables, and even in Dilworth
to proper names of six syllables, containing
such retired words as Abelbethmaacah; but
in Webster these lists proceed upon a regular gradation of pronunciation, while in Dilworth they follow such confusing and arbitrary order as is indicated by the heading,
" Words of five, six, etc., letters, viz.: two
vowels and the rest consonants; the latter
vowel serving only to lengthen the sound
of the former, except where it is otherwise
marked," which is nearly as luminous as a
direction in knitting. Each offers illustrated
fables as reading lessons, and shorter sentences are provided for first lessons in reading. In Dilworth these are, without exception, taken from the Psalms, or made up
to order to look like apocryphal psalms; in
Webster there is a suggestive divergence,
for while, as in Dilworth, the first sentence
is, " No man may put off the law of God,"
it takes a very few pages for the child to
reach the very practical passage, " As for
those boys and girls that mind not their

books, and love not church and school, but play with such as tell tales, tell lies, curse, swear, and steal, they will come to some bad end, and must be whipt till they mend their ways." The child brought up on Dilworth is practiced until nearly the last page of the work upon the lesson of the first sentence, with variations. Other differences would be suggested at once by the use of the two books. In Dilworth the child learns all manner of English proper names and abbreviations likely to be of use, such as Ldp., Bp., Rt. Wpful, Rt. Honble, Ast. P. G. C. and P. M. G. C., the last two standing, as the reader has of course already guessed, for Astronomy Professor of Gresham College, and Professor of Music at Gresham College, which we politely take to have been Tho. Dilworth's Alma Mater. In a note at the foot of the column, T. D. adds: " It argues a disrespect and slighting to use contractions to our betters." The character of this torture of the innocent was probably determined by the use for which it was intended in England, as indicated by Mr. Dilworth's dedication "To the Reverend and Worthy Promoters of the several Charity Schools in Great Britain and Ireland."

Webster's Institute, on the other hand, was plainly meant for the farmer boys and girls of his country. " The spelling-book," he says in one of his essays, " does more to form the language of a nation than all other books," and the man who first supplied our young nation with a spelling-book has undoubtedly affected its spelling habits more than any other single person. But Webster was a moralist and a philosopher as well as a speller. He was by no means restricted in his ambition to the teaching of correct spelling; he aimed to have a hand in the moulding of the national mind and the national manners. In his preface to " The American Spelling-Book," he says: " To diffuse an uniformity and purity of language in America, to destroy the provincial prejudices that originate in the trifling differences of dialect and produce reciprocal ridicule, to promote the interest of literature and the harmony of the United States, is the most earnest wish of the author, and it is his highest ambition to deserve the approbation and encouragement of his countrymen." His spelling-book, accordingly, in its early editions contained a number of

sharp little warnings in the form of foot-
notes, which imply that he seized the young
nation just in time to prevent the perpetu-
ation of vulgar errors, since these, if they
once became universal, would have compelled the hereditary Webster to make
them the basis of orthoepic canons. Thus,
ax is reprobated when *ask* is intended;
Americans were to say *wainscot*, not *winch-
cott; resin*, not *rozum; chimney*, not *chim-
bly; confiscate*, not *confisticate*. Since these
warnings disappeared after a few years it
may be presumed that he regarded the immediate danger as passed; but the more substantial matters of good morals came to
have greater prominence, and in addition
to the columns of classified words, which
constitute almost the sole contents of the
earliest edition, there came to be inserted
those fables and moral and industrial in-
junctions, with sly reminders of the virtue
of Washington, which have sunk into the
soft minds of generations of Americans.
There was a Federal catechism, and a good
deal of geographical knowledge regarding
counties and county towns, to be taken eco-
nomically in the form of spelling lessons.

The successive editions became way-marks of the progress of the nation, and so important did the book rapidly become that though its compiler was fast throwing off the bondage of Anglican spelling, he never dared to make the book conform to his own principles ; venturing only to hint in his preface at the orthographic reform which he longed to make. " The spelling," he says, " of such words as publick, favour, neighbour, head, prove, phlegm, his, give, debt, rough, well, instead of the more natural and easy method : public, favor, nabor, hed, proov, flem, hiz, giv, det, ruf, wel, has the plea of antiquity in its favor; and yet I am convinced that common sense and convenience will sooner or later get the better of the present absurd practice."

The pictures which came to bring art as an adjunct in impressing the young mind were of the order already familiar in the New England Primer, ingenuous in their simple straightforwardness and of uncompromising faithfulness to nature. The fable of the Boy that stole Apples, which I have never been able to trace back of Webster, but through him has become a part of our

mental furniture, is briskly set forth at one
of its points in a queer wood-cut. The old
man in his continental coat has only gone
as far as words, and the boy is just reaching
out his arm for the round apple near him.
If another picture had been given, the old
man's coat would have been off and that
boy would have been seen slithering down
the trunk of the tree ; and in the third
fable of the Fox and the Swallow there is a
phalanx-like arrangement of the tormenting
flies which appeals strongly to the imagina-
tion.

The second part of a Grammatical Institute was a grammar, — " a plain and comprehensive grammar founded on the true
principles and idioms of the language."
Webster had fallen upon Lowth's " Short
Introduction to the English Grammar," and
upon the basis of that book drew up his
grammar for the use of American youth.
But the principal result of his work seems
to have been the introduction of his own
mind to the study. Six years afterward
he wrote : " The favorable reception of this
prompted me to extend my original plan,
which led to a further investigation of the

principles of language. After all my reading and observation for the course of ten
years I have been able to unlearn a considerable part of what I learnt in early life,
and at thirty years of age can with confidence affirm that our modern grammars
have done much more hurt than good. The
authors have labored to prove what is ob-
viously absurd, namely, that our language
is not made right; and in pursuance of this
idea have tried to make it over again, and
persuade the English to speak by Latin
rules, or by arbitrary rules of their own.
Hence they have rejected many phrases of
pure English, and substituted those which
are neither English nor sense. Writers and
grammarians have attempted for centuries
to introduce a subjunctive mode into English, yet without effect; the language requires none distinct from the indicative;
and therefore a subjunctive form stands in
books only as a singularity, and people in
practice pay no regard to it. The people
are right, and a critical investigation of the
subject warrants me in saying that common practice, even among the unlearned,
is generally defensible on the principles of

analogy and the structure of the language, and that very few of the alterations recommended by Lowth and his followers can be vindicated on any better principle than some Latin rule or his own private opinion."

Accordingly, besides publishing some dissertations on the subject, he issued a new grammar in 1807, based this time on Horne Tooke's Diversions of Purley, an author with whom Webster would naturally be in sympathy. This grammar never had a firm hold of the public, and was subsequently incorporated into the prefatory matter of his great dictionary, where he says : " My researches into the structure of language had convinced me that some of Lowth's principles are erroneous and that my own grammar wanted material corrections. In consequence of this conviction, believing it to be immoral to publish what appeared to be false rules and principles, I determined to suppress my grammar, and actually did so."

Here we have his frankness of character, his honesty, his force of will, and the impulsiveness with which he took up attractive theories. Perhaps the most comprehensive statement of his ruling principle

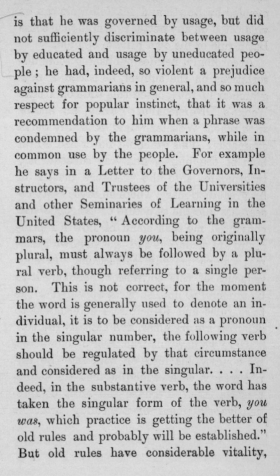

is that he was governed by usage, but did not sufficiently discriminate between usage by educated and usage by uneducated people ; he had, indeed, so violent a prejudice against grammarians in general, and so much respect for popular instinct, that it was a recommendation to him when a phrase was condemned by the grammarians, while in common use by the people. For example he says in a Letter to the Governors, Instructors, and Trustees of the Universities and other Seminaries of Learning in the United States, " According to the grammars, the pronoun *you*, being originally plural, must always be followed by a plural verb, though referring to a single person. This is not correct, for the moment the word is generally used to denote an individual, it is to be considered as a pronoun in the singular number, the following verb should be regulated by that circumstance and considered as in the singular. . . . Indeed, in the substantive verb, the word has taken the singular form of the verb, *you was*, which practice is getting the better of old rules and probably will be established." But old rules have considerable vitality, and the general opinion still is that if an individual permits himself to be represented by a plural pronoun he must accept all the grammatical consequences. " I will even venture to assert," he continues in the same letter, " that two thirds of all the corruptions in our language have been introduced by *learned* grammarians, who, from a species of pedantry acquired in schools, and from a real ignorance of the original principle of the English tongue, have been for ages attempting to correct what they have supposed *vulgar errors,* but which are in fact *established analogies.* . . . In this country it is desirable that inquiries should be free, and opinions unshackled. North America is destined to be the seat of a people more numerous probably than any nation now existing with the same vernacular language, unless one except some Asiatic nations. It would be little honorable to the founders of a great empire to be hurried prematurely into errors and corruptions by the mere force of authority."

This appeal to the pride of the young nation is a curious instance of the growing consciousness of Americanism which was

more rampant in Webster than in any of
his contemporaries. The passages which I
have been quoting intimate the deference
which Webster displayed toward the people. He was one of the first to carry a
spirit of democracy into letters. Intense
Federalist as he was, his Federalism agreed
with a stout anti-aristocratic spirit; and
throughout his work one may detect a confidence in the common sense of the people
which was as firm as Franklin's, and was
used, in his enthusiasm, to determine questions in language and literature never before
brought to such a test. Unquestionably a
main source of Webster's strength and success lay in this democratic instinct; it was
not patriotism alone, it was the spirit which
hailed the new democracy, and in its very
contempt of precedent and historic authority disclosed its rude self-reliance.

This temper had a more favorable field
for its exhibition in the third part of "A
Grammatical Institute" which bore the sub-
title: "An American Selection of Lessons
in Reading and Speaking; calculated to
improve the Minds and refine the Taste of
Youth, and also to instruct them in the

Geography, History, and Politics of the United States. To which are prefixed Rules in Elocution, and Directions for expressing the Principal Passions of the Mind." This laboriously emphatic title-page bears the motto from Mirabeau : " Begin with the infant in his cradle ; let the first word he lisps be Washington." In strict accordance with this patriotic sentiment, the compiler gives a series of lessons which would not be inappropriate to any girl or boy who in infancy had performed the feat of lisping the easy-going name which Mirabeau himself probably had some difficulty in conquering. " In the choice of pieces," says Webster in his preface, " I have been attentive to the political interests of America. I consider it as a capital fault in all our schools that the books generally used contain subjects wholly uninteresting to our youth ; while the writings that marked the Revolution, which are perhaps not inferior to the orations of Cicero and Demosthenes, and which are calculated to impress interesting truths upon young minds, lie neglected and forgotten. Several of those masterly addresses of Congress,

written at the commencement of the late
Revolution, contain such noble sentiments
of liberty and patriotism that I cannot help
wishing to transfuse them into the breasts
of the rising generation." Accordingly, he
makes abundant room in his book for orations by Hancock, Warren, Livingston, and
Joel Barlow, and for poetry by Freneau,
Dwight, Barlow, and Livingston again, all
kept in countenance by Cicero, Publius
Scipio, Shakespeare, and Pope, while a
tribute is paid to "Mr. Andrus of Yale
College, since deceased," by the insertion
of "A Dialogue written in the year 1776."
To plump from Joel Barlow at the North
Church in Hartford, July 4, 1787, to a portion of Cicero's oration against Verres, probably produced no severe shock, since both
orations were intended as exercises in speaking, and the former by its structure was removed to about the same chronological distance from the young speaker as the latter.
It would be a curious inquiry how far writers of historical addresses in America have
from the beginning been affected by the
necessity which a regard for ancient models
laid upon them of fitting the facts of our Rev-

olutionary War to oratorical periods, and how far popular conceptions of the beginning of our national life have been formed by the "pieces" which young Americans have been called upon to speak. The Roman was the most distinguished predecessor by name of this new republic, and enthusiastic patriots went to it for literary furniture as freely as their ancestors in New England applied to the Jewish theocracy. In the contemporary ephemeral literature of the time there is a faint survival of the older forms, but a more energetic reproduction of Roman symbols, taken sometimes directly from Latin literature and history, sometimes indirectly from the chill Augustan renaissance of the English eighteenth-century literature. The interior manners of the two periods are well contrasted in two sets of letters, the earlier passing between John and Margaret Winthrop, the later between John and Abigail Adams. The Scriptural allusions which crowd the Winthrop letters have not wholly disappeared in the Adams letters, but they are more formally introduced as fragmentary bits of wisdom, and appear side by side with

4

quotations from Pliny and Rollin's "Ancient
History;" Mrs. Adams signs herself Portia;
the vessels which carry the letters are the
Apollo, the Juno, and the Minerva; and
classical allusions constitute a good share of
such playfulness as may be found.

The judgment with which Webster made
his reading selections largely from American
sources was not the result of a mere Anglo-
phobia; it was the product of an ardent,
hopeful patriotism trained within narrow
provincial bounds. Webster was not old
enough to have been much under the impression of the English rule in America, and
his days had been spent in farming villages
where the traditions were little affected by
foreign life, or in a college which jumped
over intermediate centuries to find models
in Roman antiquity. His education, meaning by that the cultivation of his powers
by what were literary or circumstantial influences, had made him quite exclusively
an American and a republican; when he

began to give expression, therefore, to his
mind, he was unimpeded and unstimulated
by anything outside of the horizon of his
frugal life; he was not so much opposed

to foreign culture as he was absolutely ignorant of it; and in his career we are called upon to observe the growth of a mind as nearly native as was possible. If I am not mistaken, that which was Webster's weakness as an individual man was his strength as the pioneer of education in a new country.

CHAPTER III.

AUTHOR AND PUBLISHER.

THE second and third parts of "A Grammatical Institute" did not make Webster's fame or fortune. The first part had in it from the first the promise of success. It may fairly be called the first book published in the United States of America, and its publication, under all the conditions of business then, was a bold venture. Each State was still a law to itself, and no general act of Congress had yet been passed conferring copyright. Webster's first business before he had actually completed his spelling-book was to secure copyright laws in the several States, and he began a series of journeys to Philadelphia and the state capitals for this purpose. The history of his travels is the history of the origin of copyright laws in this country; and inasmuch as Webster has himself related in detail the steps which he took not only at this time, but later, I introduce here his statement, including in it a correspondence with Daniel Webster which has special interest at this time, when the same considerations have been urged in the renewed discussion of the subject.

" In the autumn of 1782 I rode to Philadelphia for the purpose of showing my manuscripts to gentlemen of influence, and obtaining a law for securing to authors the copyright of their publications. As the legislatures of New Jersey and Philadelphia were not then in session, the latter object could not then be accomplished. On my way I called on Governor Livingston, then in Trenton, and inquired whether it was probable that a copyright law could be obtained in New Jersey. The Governor replied that if I would wait till noon he would consult his council, then in session, and give me an answer. At the time appointed I called again, when the Governor told me the council gave him very little encouragement. In Princeton I waited on the Rev. Samuel Stanhope Smith, then professor of theology in Nassau Hall, and afterward president of that institution, who examined my manuscripts, recommended the works, and expressed his opinion in favor of copyright laws. . . .

" In October following I went to Hartford, with a view to petition the Legislature of Connecticut, then in session in that place, for a law to secure to me the copyright of my proposed book. The petition was presented, but too late in the session to obtain a hearing. I then returned to Goshen, and devoted the winter to a revision of my manuscripts, and the introduction of some improvements which had been suggested by gentlemen in Princeton and Philadelphia. In January, 1783, I prepared another memorial to be presented to the Legislature of Connecticut, for the purpose of procuring a copyright law, which memorial was committed to the care of John Canfield, Esq. But the necessity of it was superseded by the enactment of a general law upon the subject. This law was obtained by the petition of several literary gentlemen in that State.

" In the same winter I went to Kingston, in Ulster County, New York, where the legislature was in session, with a view to present a petition for the like purpose. The

necessity of such petition was prevented by
the prompt attention of General Schuyler
to my request, through whose influence a
bill was introduced into the Senate, which
at the next session became a law. In the
same winter the Legislature of Massachusetts enacted a copyright law, procured,
probably, by the agency of the Rev. Timothy Dwight, then a member of the House
of Representatives.

"As Congress, under the Confederation,
had no power to protect literary property,
several gentlemen, among whom was Joel
Barlow, presented a memorial to that body,
petitioning them to recommend to the several States the enactment of such a law.
In May, 1783, on the report of Mr. Wil-
liamson, Mr. Izard, and Mr. Madison, Congress passed a resolution, recommending to
the several States to secure to authors or
publishers of new books, not before printed,
the copyright of such books for a term not
less than fourteen years. In December,
1783, Governor Livingston informed me by
letter that the Legislature of New Jersey
had passed a law agreeable to the recommendation of Congress.

"In May, 1785, I undertook a journey to the Middle and Southern States, one object of which was to procure copyright laws to be enacted. I proceeded to Charleston, but the legislature not being in session, I returned to Baltimore, where I spent the summer. In November I visited General Washington at his mansion; he gave me letters to Governor Harrison in Richmond, and to the speakers of both houses of the legislature. The law desired was passed for securing copyrights. In December I visited Annapolis, where the legislature was in session; and in February I visited Dover, in Delaware, for the same purpose. On petition, the Legislature of Delaware appointed a committee to prepare a bill for a copyright law, just at the close of the session, but the enactment was deferred to the next session. In the year 1790 Congress enacted their first copyright law, which superseded all the state laws on the subject.

"When I was in England in 1825 I learned that the British Parliament had, a few years before, enacted a new law on copyrights, by which the rights of authors were much extended. This led me to attempt to procure a new law in the United States, giving a like extension to the rights of authors. My first attempt appears in the following letter [to the Hon. Daniel Webster, dated September 30, 1826] : —

" ' Since the celebrated decision, respecting copyright, by the highest British tribunal, it seems to have been generally admitted that an author has not a permanent and exclusive right to the publication of his original works at common law ; and that he must depend wholly on statutes for his enjoyment of that right. As I firmly believe this decision to be contrary to all our best established principles of *right* and *property*, and as I have reason to think such a decision would not now be sanctioned by the authorities of this country, I sincerely desire that while you are a member of the House of Representatives in Congress your talents may be exerted in placing this species of property on the same footing as all property, as to exclusive right and permanence of possession.

" ' Among all modes of acquiring property, or exclusive ownership, the act or operation of *creating* or *making* seems to have the first claim. If anything can justly give a man an exclusive right to the occupancy and enjoyment of a thing it must be the fact that he *made* it. The right of a farmer and mechanic to the exclusive enjoyment and right of disposal of what they *make* or *produce* is never questioned. What, then, can make a difference between the produce of *muscular strength* and the produce of the *intellect?* If it should be said that as the purchaser of a bushel of wheat has obtained not only the exclusive right to the use of it for food, but the right to sow it and increase and profit by it, let it be replied, this is true; but if he sows the wheat he must sow it on his own ground or soil. The case is different with respect to the copy of a book, which a purchaser has obtained, for the copyright is the *author's soil*, which the purchaser cannot legally occupy.

" ' Upon what principles, let me ask, can any fellow-citizens declare that the production of the farmer and the artisan shall be protected by common law, or the principles of natural and social rights, without a special statute, and without paying a premium for the enjoyment of their property, while they declare that I have only a temporary right to the fruits of my labor, and even this cannot be enjoyed without giving a premium? Are such principles as these consistent with the established doctrines of property, and of moral right and wrong among an enlightened people? Are such principles consistent with the high and honorable notions of justice and equal privileges which our citizens claim to entertain and to cherish, as characteristic of modern improvements in civil society? How can the *recent origin* of a particular species of property vary the principles of ownership? I say nothing of the inexpedience of such a policy, as it regards the discouragement of literary exertions. Indeed, I can probably say nothing on this subject that you have not said or thought; at least I presume you have often contemplated this subject in all its bearings.

"'The British Parliament, about ten or twelve years ago, passed a new act on this subject, giving to authors and proprietors of new works an absolute right to the exclusive use of the copyright for twenty-eight years, with some other provisions which I

do not recollect ; but the act makes or continues the condition that the author or proprietor shall deposit *eleven copies* of the
work in Stationers' Hall, for the benefit of
certain public libraries. This premium will
often amount to *fifty pounds sterling*, or
more. An effort was made by publishers
to obtain a repeal of this provision ; but it
was opposed by the institutions which were
to receive the benefit, and the attempt
failed.

"'I have a great interest in this question,
and I think the interest of science and literature in this question are by no means inconsiderable. I sincerely wish our legislature would come at once to the line of right
and justice on this subject, and pass a new
act, the preamble to which shall admit the
principle that an author has, by common
law, or natural justice, the sole and *permanent* right to make profit by his own labor,
and that his heirs and assigns shall enjoy
the right unclogged with conditions. The
act thus admitting the right would prescribe
only the *mode* by which it shall be ascer-
tained, secured, and enjoyed, and violations
of the right punished ; and perhaps make

some provisions for the case of attempts to elude the statute by slight alterations of books by mutilations and transpositions.'

" To this letter Mr. Webster returned the following answer : —

" ' Boston, *October* 14, 1826.

" ' Dear Sir, — I have received yours of the 30th of September, and shall, with your permission, lay it before the committee of the judiciary next session, as that committee has in contemplation some important changes in the law respecting copyright. Your opinion, in the abstract, is certainly right and uncontrovertible. Authorship is, in its nature, ground of property. Most people, I think, are as well satisfied (or better) with the reasoning of Mr. Justice Yates as with that of Lord Mansfield in the great case of Miller and Taylor. But after all, property, in the social state, must be the creature of law ; and it is a question of expediency, high and general, not particular expediency, how and how far the rights of authorship should be protected. I confess frankly that I see, or think I see, objections to make it perpetual. At the same time I am willing to extend it further than at present, and am fully persuaded that it ought to be relieved from all charges, such as depositing copies, etc.

        " ' Yours,   D. WEBSTER.'

" In the autumn of 1827 I applied to the Hon. Mr. Ingersoll, a representative from Connecticut, stating to him the facts of an extension of copyright in Great Britain, as also in France, and requesting him to use his influence to have a bill for a new law brought forward in Congress. Mr. Ingersoll very cheerfully complied. On the 17th December, on the motion of Mr. Ingersoll, the House of Representatives ' *Resolved,* that the committee on the judiciary inquire into the expediency of extending the time for which copyrights may be hereafter secured to authors, beyond the period now allowed by law; and also of affording further protection to authors against the publication of abridgments or summaries of works, after the copyrights thereof have been secured.' As the committee delayed several weeks to make a report, Mr. Ingersoll conversed fully on the subject with one of the members, and addressed a note to the committee, in which he stated the provision of the British Statute 34th Geo. III., enlarging the rights of authors, and the liberal provisions of the French laws on the subject. He stated some of the defects of the old law of the United States, and urged the expediency and justice of a more liberal law.

" A petition signed by many respectable literary men was, about this time, presented to Congress, praying for the same object. Some members of the committee were opposed to the measure; but at length, on the first of February, 1828, the committee reported a bill consisting of three sections only, extending the term of copyrights from fourteen to twenty-eight years, and securing the benefit of the act to authors who had previously obtained a copyright under the old law. On the 21st of February, Mr. Verplanck submitted to the House of Representatives an amendment to the bill reported by the committee, entitled an 'Amendment to a Bill to amend and consolidate the Acts respecting Copyrights.' This amendment was printed by order of the House. It was intended to embrace all the material provisions of the two former laws, and those of the bill reported by the judiciary committee ; it contained also some additional improvements. Nothing further was done, and the bill and amendment died at the close of the session.

"At the next session (1829–1830) the Hon. Mr. Ellsworth, a member from Connecticut, was appointed one of the judiciary committee, of which the Hon. Mr. Buchanan was chairman. Before Mr. Ellsworth left home, I applied to him to make efforts to procure the enactment of a new copyright law, and sent a petition to Congress, praying for the renewal of the copyright of one of my books. This petition, being referred to the judiciary committee, brought the subject distinctly into consideration. After consultation, the committee authorized Mr. Ellsworth to prepare a bill for a general law on the subject. In order to present the subject in its true light to the committee and to Congress, Mr. Ellsworth wrote notes to the ministers of the principal European nations, requesting information from each of them respecting the state of copyrights in the nations they represented. From their answers, and an inspection of the laws of some of the governments, Mr. Ellsworth framed a report, stating the terms of time for which copyrights are secured to authors in Great Britain, France, Russia, Sweden, Denmark, and certain states in Germany. He also framed a bill for a law intended to embrace all the material provisions of the old laws with those of the bill reported by the former judiciary committee.

" In this bill Mr. Ellsworth introduced some valuable provisions which had been omitted in the old laws, and in the bill and amendment offered at the former session. He also obtained from his friends some suggestions which enabled him to correct some errors and supply defects. This bill was approved by the judiciary committee, reported by Mr. Ellsworth, and printed by order of the House. But such was the pressure of business, and so little interest was felt in the bill, that no efforts of Mr. Ellsworth could bring it before the House at that session.

" Finding the efforts of the friends of the bill in Congress to be unavailing to obtain a hearing, I determined in the winter of

1830–1831 to visit Washington myself, and
endeavor to accomplish the object. Accordingly I took lodgings at the seat of government, where I passed nine or ten weeks;
and during this time read a lecture in the
Hall of the Representatives, which was well
attended, and, as my friends informed me,
had no little effect in promoting the object
of obtaining a law for securing copyrights.

"The difficulties which had prevented
the bill from being brought forward now
disappeared. The bill, at the second reading in the House of Representatives, met
with some opposition; but it was ably supported by Mr. Ellsworth, Mr. Verplanck,
and Mr. Huntington. It passed to a third
reading by a large majority, and was or-
dered to be engrossed without opposition.
When the bill came before the Senate, it
was referred to the judiciary committee.
Mr. Rowan, the chairman, being absent, the
committee requested the Hon. Daniel Webster to take the bill, examine it, and report
it if he thought proper; he did so, and under
all circumstances deemed it expedient to report it without amendment. On the second reading Mr. Webster made a few ex-

planatory remarks: no other person uttered
a word on the subject; and it passed to a
third reading by a unanimous vote. On the
third reading, the Senate, on motion, dis-
pensed with the reading, and it passed to
be engrossed, without debate.

"In my journeys to effect this object,
and in my long attendance in Washington,
I expended nearly a year of time. Of my
expenses in money I have no account, but
it is a satisfaction to me that a liberal statute for securing to authors the fruit of their
labor has been obtained."

In this summary the whole history of the
copyright statutes appears, and it is interesting to note that the earliest action by
the States and Congress received its impulse
from Webster's spelling-book; the later and
final form of the law was adopted in connection with Mr. Webster's indefatigable
efforts, and the first book to take advantage
of it was his "American Dictionary." His
keen sense of the business relations of his
literary work is seen in this early and late
energy in securing satisfactory copyright
laws. It is noticeable, too, that in his cor-

respondence with Daniel Webster he took the position which has of late been held as the only solution of all copyright questions. Noah Webster may not have been a great man in his generation, but he had a singular faculty of being the first in time in many departments of literary industry, and constantly to have anticipated other people.

Wherever he went he showed the rough draft of his book; he assailed members of Congress and men of eminence generally. He had faith in it, and he lived at a time when the individual testimony of men was of greater weight than now. There were no organs of literary or educational opinion, no academies or bodies of men especially esteemed as juries in the case of any book on trial, and indorsements were looked for as essential to the success of any new venture. There was no great public to show its interest by buying, and there were no publishers of capital and organization to relieve the author of publishing labor. In the recently published correspondence of Jeremy Belknap and Ebenezer Hazard,[1] one may read the difficulties encountered

1 *Belknap Papers,* v., Coll. Mass. Hist. Soc. iii.

by a scholarly man in getting his historical work published. The correspondence for two years between these gentlemen, with reference to the publication of Belknap's "History of New Hampshire," a volume of five hundred pages, shows that every detail of paper, print, and binding, and almost all arrangements for securing subscriptions, fell upon the author and his friend, acting for and with him. Subscribers were sought with painful endeavor, one at a time, and all the points at issue were discussed in letters which seemed sometimes to travel by chance.

Webster, without money, and almost without friends, but with the kind of faith which works miracles with other people's faith, succeeded at length in persuading Hudson & Goodwin, printers in Hartford, to issue an edition of five thousand copies of the spelling-book. John Trumbull and Joel Barlow were his chief supporters, the latter backing him with a little money. The printer was the publisher then; and an author, in making his arrangements, was accustomed to sell the right to print and publish to various printers in various parts of the country, — a custom which continued through the first quarter of the century. The isolation of the several settled communities rendered collision between the several dealers unlikely; and, in the absence of quick communication, no place had any advantage except as a dépôt for the neighboring district. Rights to print were granted for fourteen years. Such a contract was made in 1818 by Webster with Mr. Hudson, who was to pay $3,000 a year during the term. The reader will recall similar arrangements in Irving's ventures. The popularity of the speller rendered it liable to piracy, especially in the ruder parts of the country, and as late as 1835 Mr. Webster writes to his son, established as a bookseller in Louisville: "I would suggest whether it would not be advisable to publish in Kentucky, or at least in Tennessee, a short note like this: ' The Public are cautioned against buying " Webster's American Spelling-Book;" the editions now in the market are pirated, badly printed, and incorrect. The author expressly disclaims them.' "

The final success of the little book has

been quite beyond definite computation, but a few figures will show something of the course it has run. In 1814, 1815, the sales averaged 286,000 copies a year; in 1828 the sales were estimated to be 350,000 copies. In 1847 the statement was made that about twenty-four million copies of the book had been published up to that time, and that the sale was then averaging a million of copies a year. It was also then said, that during the twenty years in which he was employed in compiling his "American Dictionary," the entire support of his family was derived from the profits of this work, at a premium for copyright of five mills a copy. The sales for eight years following the Civil War, namely, 1866-1873, aggregated 8,196,028; and the fact that the average yearly sale was scarcely greater than in 1847 may be referred in part to the great enterprise in the publication of school-books, which has marked the last twenty years, by which his speller has been one only of a great many, in part, also, to the impoverishment of the South where Webster's book had been more generally accepted than at the North.

The great demand that there was for elementary school-books, the real advance of Webster's over any then existing, the promptness with which he met the first call, all these causes combined to give a great impetus to the little book. At first sight there seems something amusing in the importance which not only Webster but other men of the time attached to the spelling-book. Timothy Pickering, in camp at Newburgh, waiting for the final word of disbanding, sat up into the night to read it! " By the eastern post yesterday," he writes to his wife, " I was lucky enough to receive the new spelling-book [Webster's] I mentioned in my last, and instead of sleeping (for I had a waking fit which prevented me), I read it through last night, except that I only examined a part of the different tables. I am much pleased with it. The author is ingenious, and writes from his own experience as a school-master, as well as the best authorities ; and the time will come when no authority, as an English grammarian, will be superior to his own. It is the very thing I have so long wished for, being much dissatisfied with any spelling-book I had seen before. I now send you the book, and request you to let John take it to his master, with the enclosed letter ; for I am determined to have him instructed upon this new, ingenious, and, at the same time, easy plan. There are, you will see by the Introduction, two more parts to come to complete the plan. I am a stranger to Mr. Webster, but I intend, when I can find leisure, to write him on the subject, using the liberty (which he requests) to suggest some little matters which may be altered and improved in his next edition, for I think the work will do honor to his country, and I wish it may be perfect. Many men of literature might think it too trifling a subject ; but I am of a different opinion, and am happy that a gentleman of Mr. Webster's genius and learning has taken it up. All men are pleased with an elegant pronunciation, and this new Spelling-Book shows children how to acquire it with ease and certainty." [1]

Pickering's letter helps us to get behind " Webster's Spelling-Book " in 1783, instead of looking at it from this later vantage-

[1] *Life of Timothy Pickering,* i. 479, 480.

ground of an accumulated American literature. There runs through the correspondence of that day a tone which we easily call provincial, but is nevertheless a distinct expression of the consciousness of the young nation. The instinct of literature is toward self-centring, and the sense of national being was very strong in men who had been giving their days and nights to the birth of a new nation. To understand the state of things in 1783 we should look at the literary ventures, inclusive of educational, within the boundaries of the Southern States during the War of 1861-1865. There the interruption of commerce with the North compelled a resort to home production in school-book literature, and intensity of feeling upon sectional questions found frequent expression in spelling-books and arithmetics. "Webster's Elementary" was reprinted at Macon, without illustrations and some of the diacritical marks, *mutatis mutandis*. The reader finds the morals of the book and the earlier patriotism unchanged, but remembers its latitude when he reads: " The Senate of the Confederate States is called the Upper House of Congress : The

President of the Confederate States is elective once every six years : The Confederate States have a large extent of sea-coast, and many parts of the Confederate States are noted for the fertility of the soil." But these are innocent adaptations ; one must look to the arithmetics for sectional feeling.

In Webster's time, men whose lives had been spent in the struggle for independence and autonomy looked upon everything relating to their country with a concentration of interest which not only attested the sincerity of their convictions, but made them indifferent to the larger, more universal standards. They were seeing things with American, not European eyes. When Dr. Belknap and his friend Mr. Hazard were carefully arranging for the publication of the "History of New Hampshire," they made proposals to the Longmans, in London, to take an edition, without any apparent suspicion that such a book might lack readers in England. The publishers' polite reply intimates the "apprehension that the history of one particular province of New England would not be of sufficient importance to engage the attention of this coun-

try, and particularly as it is at present
brought down no lower than the year 1714."
Belknap's History is an admirable piece of
work, the first scholarly work of its kind
on this side of the water, and Dr. Belknap
respected his book. To him, as to many of
that generation, a book was a serious undertaking, and each new one that came was
carefully weighed and its character measured ; a history of New Hampshire was not
a mere piece of local self-complacency, but a
dignified adventure into a portion of American history hitherto unexplored. The work
expended upon it was as careful and grave
as if the subject had been the Peloponne-
sian War. Indeed, one of the substantial
evidences of the historic justification of the
war for independence is to be found in the
alacrity with which the scholarly element
in the country busied itself about themes
which were close at hand and connected
with the land of their life.

Literature in its finer forms had but slender encouragement. The absence of easy
communication, the poverty of the people,
the dispersion of the population, gave little
chance for bookstores and circulating libra-

ries and private accumulation. It must not
be forgotten, either, that the era of cheap
books had not yet come in England, and
that the periodical form was still in embryo.
To look back on one of the rather juiceless
periodicals which sprang up so frequently
at the beginning of our literature because
they had no depth of earth, and withered
away rootless and sunstruck, is to be over-
taken half with scorn for their pretense,
and half with pity for conductors and readers, who had to make believe very hard to
find them quite nice. "They would bear a
little more seasoning certainly," like the
marchioness's orange-peel and water ; yet
how strong must have been the passion for
literature when money was expended and
pains taken with these hopeless ventures.
The change in popular taste, moreover, must
not mislead us into supposing that writings
which are arid to us now were necessarily
devoid of interest to contemporary readers.
We take down from the shelf the solitary
volume which contains the "American Magazine," and its reading-matter looks as faded
to our eyes as the leather upon the covers,
but it was once the latest publication of the

day. We can with little difficulty imagine
that the monthly report of Warren Hast-
ings' trial, with its plan of the High Court
at Westminster, would have an interest at
the time quite as reasonable in its way as
that which held readers of journals, not so
long extinct, over the details of the Tich-
borne case. It is in the field of polite literature that our later taste refuses to discover
anything in common with the readers of the
" American Magazine." What impresses
one most in such a periodical is the value
which the conductors set upon American
historical material. This was offered to the
public with all the assurance which now at-
tends the promise of a great serial story.
The explanation may most reasonably be
found in the fact, that the subscribers to
any such magazine at the time must have
been sought among the well educated, and
this class had been used chiefly to a serious
view of literature.

The " American Magazine" was Webster's venture, and in the Belknap and Hazard correspondence one may find some curious incidents in the struggle for existence
which the magazine had. It should be pre-

mised that neither of these gentlemen —
and they represented the most cultivated
class of the day — had much confidence in
Webster. They nicknamed him the "Monarch," possibly from some assumption and
arrogance in his tone, and he is rarely mentioned by them except in a slighting manner. "*I* think the *Monarch* a literary
puppy, from what little I have seen of him,"
writes Hazard to Belknap. "He certainly
does not want understanding, and yet there
is a mixture of self-sufficiency, all-sufficiency,
and at the same time a degree of insufficiency about him, which is (to me) intoler-
able. I do *not* believe that he is fit for a
superintendent ; that the persons mentioned
will be his coadjutors, or that either the *demand* or the *profits* will be any way near
equal to his expectations. His specimens
already published [three numbers of the
'American Magazine'] are below medioc-
rity, and even in them *he* is too much the
hero of the tale. His *plan* of a *Federal*
publication, if sensible, judicious men could
be engaged to execute it, and an editor of
the same stamp could be procured, I think
would do well. *Considering circumstances,*

I would not advise you to engage with him,
but I think you may avail yourself of his
application with the Columbians ; only take
care to do it in such a way that you may
not, between two stools, fall to the ground."

The " Columbian " was a magazine of a
little older standing to which Dr. Belknap
had been contributing (his " Foresters "
appeared there), and the incident of the
worldly-wise Hazard, gently encouraging the
clergyman to play the rivals against each
other, has at least an approach to modern
literary history. Webster, with his restlessness, had no sooner launched the " American Magazine" than he began to form other
projects, as intimated in Hazard's letter,
and wished to secure not only Belknap's
pen, but his more active partnership. Hazard writes again to his friend, after being
asked for further advice : " I am really at
a loss how to advise you, but think, upon
the whole, I would let the Columbians know
that ' my necessities also compelled the making a close bargain ; ' that I had been applied to in behalf of the New York magazine, but felt myself so much interested in
their success (having been so long connected

with them) that I did not like to leave
them, provided they would stipulate to allow me, *certainly*, what I deemed a reasonable compensation for my assistance, which
they acknowledge they do not now allow;
and that, upon their doing this, I would continue to aid them. If you can contribute
the stipulated assistance to them in case you
accept N. W.'s proposal, I see no reason
why you should not do the latter too; for,
if you fulfill your engagements, you do them
no injustice. You may, in this case, as well
have two strings to your bow as not, and I
think I would advise to it, especially as the
' Columbian's ' continuance is uncertain.[1] I
would inform N. W. that some consideration was necessary respecting his plan ; but
that I was, upon the whole, inclined to think
I would join him, if he could get the other
gentlemen he mentioned to me to be concerned. I think no *cash* is to be advanced
by you, upon his plan. It will be some
months before he can begin, and I would
not exclude myself from a chance."

Dr. Belknap's letters to Webster unfortu-

---

[1] Nothing in these periodical ventures seems so certain
as their uncertainty.

nately do not appear, but his friend, through
whom he wrote, commends him for his prudence. " I find," he writes, " you have not
a more exalted idea of the Monarch than I
have. I should not be fond of a connection
with him, unless I saw it clearly to my interest." He praises him also for his exertions in behalf of the feeble " Columbian,"
which owed its life to him, in his opinion.
Oddly enough, after all of Hazard's cautions
and advice to Belknap, he seems himself to
have been involved in negotiations with
Webster, and from this point the correspondence has more interest as throwing
light upon the estimation in which literary
material was held at the time. Mr. Hazard
had for a long time been making a collection
of papers bearing upon American colonial
history, and had not seen his way clear to a
profitable publication of them. Noah Webster suddenly appears as the agent for a
new magazine in which he has a slight interest, and makes proposals to Mr. Hazard.
It is amusing to see how shy Hazard is of
any close connection with Webster, and yet
how continually Webster appears in the
foreground in the affair.

"What would you think," writes Hazard to Belknap, "of my collection of papers coming to light after lying in obscurity so long? It is likely to be the case. The 'American Magazine' is to appear in a new form,[1] and on an extensive plan, and to be the property of *a society* of gentlemen, among whom N. W. holds but one share; and I am told he is going to remove from hence [New York] to Connecticut, so that he will not be the editor. Their plan is to publish one hundred and four pages monthly, fifty-six of them are to be in the usual magazine style, twenty-four are to contain State Papers, and twenty-four either historical *MSS.*, such as 'Winthrop's Journal,' or a republication of ancient, valuable, and scarce American histories, such as Smith's of Virginia, etc., etc. N. W. called, to know if I would dispose of my collection for this purpose, informing me that they intended to print in such a way that the State Papers and histories might be detached from the magazine and bound by themselves. After considering of the matter, I concluded to let them have the collection for £500, which

[1] It was now in its last number for the year.

they agreed to give. I don't altogether like
this way of publishing the papers; but when
I reflected on the great uncertainty of my
being able to publish them at all, the risque
I run by their remaining *in statu quo*, and
the little probability that I should clear
£500 by them if I should publish, I thought
it best to say yes. The money is to be paid
by installments. All this is *inter nos*."

Dr. Belknap now had an opportunity to
repay his friend's favors in kind, and in
acknowledging the letter just quoted he
writes : " I could wish that you would take
off the restriction of secrecy, so far as it
relates to the intended publication of the
magazine and its appendage, because I apprehend it may be in my power to set on
foot a similar publication here ; and the
knowledge that such a design is on foot
elsewhere may prove a stimulus to the undertaking." He prudently remarks that
the sale made by his friend is good, " provided the purchasers do not fail in the pay-
ment." Hazard returns to the matter in
his next letter : " With respect to the *MSS.*
I made a pretty *safe* bargain, and yet much
will depend on the success of the publica-

tion as to the *quickness* of the pay. . . . By
agreement I am to hand my papers out
in monthly portions, and in chronological
order. The January magazine, or rather
Register, is to contain twenty-four pages of
them, and as many of 'Winthrop's Journal.'
The design of the intended publication is no
secret now, having been advertised in the
newspapers; but I write you not to say anything about what I am to have for my
papers. . . . N. W. had printed six sheets
of Winthrop, but, upon the new plan's strik-
ing him, he thought it best to publish in
the new mode; and I am told he will lose
his expense so far, for his paper is not so
fine as the new work is to be done upon,
inter nos."

Suddenly Hazard writes to Belknap that
Webster is likely to call upon him, and that
if he offers him a partnership in the new
magazine, he is not at once to decline. It
is not worth while to follow the ins and
outs of the correspondence upon a scheme
which finally fell through, but a full letter from Hazard to Belknap may fairly be
drawn from, since it puts one into tolerably
complete possession of the whole story.

" You must know that N. W. has been
for some time trying to get my State Papers published, and he has generally proposed it in such a way as to have a share
in them himself. Several plans were proposed, and at last the idea of the Register
was started. He called on me and told me
that he had been speaking with some other
gentlemen about being concerned in the
' American Magazine,' and that they were
to be concerned with him. He informed me
of their plan, and wished me to join them,
and that my papers might be published in
the Register. He intimated that he had
five hundred subscribers [to the ' American
Magazine '] who would continue to take the
new work, and that the improvement proposed would greatly increase the number
of subscribers. I objected against being a
partner, but had no objection against let-
ting them have my papers for £500. After
a variety of negotiations, I consented to become a partner, — and they agreed to allow
me £500 for my papers, to be paid out of
the profits of the publication, — if they
would yield me £50 per annum, at least,
clear of my share of all expenses; if not, the

other proprietors were to make up that sum
to me annually ; and, should the work be
discontinued before I was paid, they were
then to pay me as much as with my profits
(all expenses first deducted) would make
£500. Regular written articles were drawn,
and executed by all but one partner, who
has not yet signed them, nor will, 'til he
sees such a number of subscribers in this
city [New York] and its vicinity as will defray the actual expense of the work. The
profits he is willing to risque. He is a discreet, sensible man, and will be what the
sailors call our *main stay.* After the articles
were executed, some of the proprietors observed that they had given their bond to
me for £500, which must be paid at all
events, and that I was to run no risque,
and, in fact, to pay no expense, — which
was not putting matters on a fair footing
with respect to them (before the time the
proposals were published). They came
and stated the case to me. I immediately
saw the propriety of their remarks, and
without hesitation agreed to a new article,
that their bond for the price of my papers
should not be in force immediately *upon*

their publishing (which was the case before), but that they might publish for three
months; if they then discontinued the publication, the bond was to be of no effect;
if they continued it after that period, it was
to be in full force; and I agreed to furnish
my proportion of the State Papers, *i. e.*,
that, as there were four proprietors, the
others should pay me but £375, — the remaining £125 being my proportion of the
cost of the papers. Thus relief was given
on equitable principles.

"In the course of our conversations, at
different times, *writers* were talked of; N.
W. mentioned you. I agreed that you
would be a very suitable person, if you
could be got to engage in it, but was ap-
prehensive your situation would not admit
of it. N. W. had no doubt you could be
engaged, for he was very confident (or well
persuaded, or something of that kind) that
you wrote for the 'Columbian,' and were
paid for it; and he ascribed the biographical pieces, in particular, to you. Upon my
asking the reasons of his opinion, he replied
that he did not know (or believe) that anybody else possessed suitable materials; but

I suspect he has had more particular information in Philadelphia. It was suggested among the proprietors that Thomas's magazine [1] would interfere with us in Massachusetts, where we hope for a number of subscribers; and N. W. afterwards hinted to me the idea of a coalition, which I was pleased with. He told me he was going to the eastward, and would talk with Thomas about it. I *supposed* that he would talk with *you* too, and gave you the hint that you might be prepared. It seems he has done so; and by last post I received proposals for an union, which I have laid before the proprietors here, and they are disapproved of. Upon this plan, the *Register* was to be printed here, and the *Magazine* in Boston. One of the proprietors here was to furnish half the matter for the magazine monthly, and forward it to Boston, where N. W. was to act as editor, or engage Mr. Belknap, or some person of equal ability, to act for him; and this editor was to furnish the other half of the matter. As a compensation for my papers, I was to be

---

[1] The *Massachusetts Magazine*, shortly after commenced by Isaiah Thomas.

a proprietor of a seventh of both publications, for they were to be separate. All
expenses, bad debts, and other losses were
to be divided equally among the partners.
These proposals were signed by Noah Webster and Isaiah Thomas & Co. In a letter
to me, N. W. sent a calculation, by which he
attempted to prove that the value of a share
would be near £200 per annum. Such an
hint might have done for a person unac-
quainted with the nature of the business,
but old birds want a more substantial temptation than chaff. A principal objection
against the plan of union was the risque
and expense of sending materials and publications backwards and forwards through
so great a distance: one failure would be
fatal to one month's magazine, and a repe-
tition of such a disaster would discourage
subscribers. The subscribers here would
probably not be satisfied with a magazine
printed elsewhere, and could not be furnished with one so early in the month;
and, for my part, I am not willing to give
up my papers on so precarious a chance of
a recompense.

" N. W. (notwithstanding his obligation

under hand and seal) confesses himself unwilling to continue the Magazine and Register on our first plan ; and I am much mistaken if the other proprietors do not disap-
point him by taking him at his word and
releasing him from his obligations; for his
being known to be concerned makes the
subscription go on heavily (this *inter nos*).
His magazine was a paltry performance,
and people fear a continuation of it. We
cannot find his five hundred subscribers yet.
We have but about two hundred in this
city, most of whom have been tempted by
my papers, as is said. We agreed among
ourselves not to let the proprietors be
known, but N. W. has let the cat quite out
of the bag. I am clear for going on without him, which I think may be done better
than with him ; and my plan would be that
a sufficient number of literary characters
should be united to make the most, if not
the whole, of the magazine *original*. The
profits upon each share (especially at first)
would be but small ; but so, on the other
hand, would be the risque. Suppose there
should be *no* profit for a year or two, and
that the work should but barely defray the

expense for that time, yet it may be presumed that, if it was conducted with spirit, the public would patronize it, being sure of original entertainment, and that at length the property would become very valuable. What do you think of this idea?"

Dr. Belknap's reply to this letter is the last reference to the project which has any interest: "The Monarch called upon me last Monday evening, when I was abroad, and left word that he should come again next day at noon, *upon business*. The *real* business was to fish out what I had heard from you. I had then received only your short letter, and told him that I had heard nothing. He talked about the magazine, and about my being a partner, and about the business of an editor, and about his being a lawyer (which, by the way, was new to me), and about the value of a share, which, as he then estimated it, would be from £50 to £100 per annum, etc., etc., but expected to hear from you and the proprietors more particularly by the next post, and then we were to have a farther conference. The next post brought me your long letter, and he has not made his appearance since. I suppose, by what you say in *confidence* to me, that he finds he cannot be director general, and possibly suspects that he may have very little to do. I find myself under some embarrassment with regard to this *personage*. However, as he is going to marry into a family with some branches of which I have long had a very agreeable connection, I must suffer myself to be in a degree of acquaintance with him, especially if (as he *threatens*) he should make this place [Boston] his future residence. If I cannot esteem him as a friend, I do not wish to make him an enemy, and I am very awkward in the art of Chesterfield. Hence arises my embarrassment. What he has told Thomas I know not, but I must do him the justice to say that he did not tell me the names of any of the proprietors, excepting yourself and himself; nor do I know who the others are."

Hazard's papers were finally published by themselves, and the Magazine and Register never got beyond the proposals point. Before the collection was published, however, another magazine loomed up, for the regular failure of each venture never seemed to dampen the ardor of magazine projectors. The story of the enterprise sketched in these letters may be taken as the story of all, — sanguine literary men and inert subscribers; a class of material is reckoned upon which always seems abundant, vastly interesting to the persons who hold it, but insufficient to beguile subscribers. Mr. Hazard, with his collection of papers, expects five hundred pounds, and his associates think him not unreasonable, especially after he agrees to pay one fourth himself; and with all his prudence and shrewdness he begins to count on the profits of the magazine with something of Webster's facile hope.

Webster himself, in spite of the dislike with which Hazard and Belknap agreed to regard him, appears in an honorable light. No doubt he was consequential and eager to have a hand in what was going on, but he had the confidence and courage which seem to have been lacking in his associates. His impulsive dashes at literature and capricious excursions into the realms of language were offensive to highly conservative and orderly scholars like these correspondents, and they sniffed at him rather con-

temptuously; but Webster could disregard
the criticism of others when he had such
unbounded self-reliance and zeal. He did
not count the cost carefully of what he undertook, but allowed himself the luxury of
seizing at once upon what engaged his interest. The publication of " Winthrop's
Journal," referred to in the correspondence,
was an undertaking which a more scholarly
man might have set about with greater care
and deliberation. Webster never read the
original. He saw a copy from it in the
possession of Governor Trumbull, and, per-
ceiving the value of the material, made
haste to get it published. He employed a
secretary of the governor, who made a copy
of the copy, comparing it with the original,
which Webster had never seen. Mr. Sav-
age, the learned editor of the Journal in its
complete form, sarcastically says : " The
celebrated philologist, *who in his English
Dictionary triumphed over the difficulties* of
derivation in our etymology from Danish,
Russian, Irish, Welsh, German, high or low,
Sanscrit, Persian, or Chaldee fountains,
might, after exhausting his patience, have
reputably shrunk from encounter with the

manuscript of Winthrop." But it was
something for Webster to have succeeded
in securing a publication of the book in
1790, and the credit due him is not lessened
by the fact that he risked his whole property in the enterprise, and lost money.

He was at this time far from being settled
in life. For half a dozen years he had been
scrambling along as well as he could, teaching, lecturing, practicing a little law, working his books, writing for the newspapers,
securing the passage of copyright laws, trying this city and that with new ventures,
none of which gave him a subsistence.
Meanwhile, he had met in Philadelphia a
Boston lady, whom his diary shows him to
have followed with the zeal of his ardent
nature; and it is not to be wondered at that
he carried his point here, as so often elsewhere, and settled, as he thought at the
time, in Hartford, in 1789, with his wife,
Rebecca, daughter of Mr. William Green-
leaf, of Boston. His brief account of himself at this date was in the summary: "I
had an enterprising turn of mind, was bold,
vain, and inexperienced." John Trumbull,
writing to Oliver Wolcott, announces that

" Webster has returned, and brought with him a pretty wife. I wish him success, but I doubt, in the present decay of business in our profession [the law], whether his profits will enable him to keep up the style he sets out with. I fear he will breakfast upon Institutes, dine upon Dissertations, and go to bed supperless." The breakfast was indeed likely to prove the only substantial meal; how substantial it proved we have already noticed. No doubt Webster appeared to his friends, as half to himself, a restless, uneasy man, incapable of steady application to law, and making hazardous ventures in literature in that combined character of author and publisher which the circumstances of the time rendered almost necessary to any one who undertook to make a profession of letters.

It is a little significant of Webster's relation to literature that he moved outside of the knot of men known in our literary history as the Hartford wits. So many recent claimants for the position of democratic jester have engaged the public attention that the Hartford wits who amused our grandfathers rest their fame now rather

7

upon tradition than upon any perennial live-
liness. By their solitude in the pages of
American literature their very title has acquired a certain gravity, and we are apt
to regard them with respect rather than
to read them for amusement. Fossil wits
seem properly to be classed with the formation from which they are dug, and not
with living types of the same order. Yet
no picture of the times in which Webster
lived would be complete without a slight
reminiscence of this coterie, and the fact
that Webster was the neighbor of these
men and himself living by letters suggests
a fresh illustration of the truth that kinship
in literature is something finer and closer
than mere circumstantial neighborliness.
Trumbull, Hopkins, Alsop, Dwight, and the
minor stars in this twinkling galaxy, were
staunch Federalists, and the occasion of their
joint efforts was chiefly political, but Webster's Federalism did not give him a place
in the set.

The " Echo " was the title which the wits
gave to a series of satires that mocked the
prose of the day. If an editor published a
piece of bloated writing, the bubble was

pricked by the poetical version ; if a politi-
cian disclosed his weakness, his words were
caught up and made to turn him into ridicule. The wits were on the lookout for
humbug in any quarter, but they had their
pet aversions, Sam Adams and the Jaco-
bins being oftenest pilloried. A bombastic
account of a thunder-storm in Boston appears to have given occasion for the first
skit, and it was scarcely necessary to do
more than parody the grandiloquent newspaper language. " The clouds soon dissipated, and the appearance of the azure
vault left trivial hopes of further need-
ful supplies from the uncorked bottles of
heaven. In a few moments the horizon
was again overshadowed, and an almost im-
penetrable gloom mantled the face of the
skies. . . . The majestic roar of disploded
thunders, now bursting with a sudden crash,
and now wasting the rumbling ECHO of their
sounds in other lands, added indescribable
grandeur to the sublime scene." The suggestion of the " Echo " came from this
phrase, and the success of the first venture
easily directed the writers into the use of
their instrument for lashing political ene-

mies. Two numbers were given to matters
of trivial or temporary interest, and then
there was a shot at a piece of fustian in
the "Boston Argus" on Liberty, followed
shortly after by a gibe at some correspond-
ent of the " Argus," who frantically ex-
claimed, on the occasion of a town meeting
refusing to hear Sam Adams: "Shall Europe hear, shall our Southern brethren be
told, that Samuel Adams rose to speak in
the midst of his fellow-citizens, and was silenced!" A few lines from this satire will
best illustrate the vigorous treatment which
the wits employed, and the gusto with
which they jostled the great Democrat: —

" Shall Europe hear, shall Gallia's king be told,
That Prince so spirited, so wise and bold,
Whose duteous subjects, anxious to improve
On common forms of loyalty and love,
Took from their sovereign's hands the reins of state,
For fear his royal nerves could not support the weight ?
And shall our worthy brethren of the South
Be told Sam Adams could not ope his mouth ?
That mouth whence streams of elocution flowed,
Like tail of saw-mill, rapid, rough, and loud,
Sweet as the honey-dews that Maia pours
O'er her green forests and her tufts of flowers, —
That potent mouth, whence issued words of force
To stun an ox, or terrify a horse.
Be told that while those brats whose feeble sight

But just had oped on Freedom's dawning light,
Born in the nick of time that bliss to know
Which to his great and mighty toils we owe,
Received applause from Sages, Fools, and Boys,
The mighty Samuel could not make a noise?
Be told that, silenced by their clam'rous din,
He vainly tried one word to dove-tail in;
That though he strove to speak with might and main
His voice and strivings equally were vain?

   .   .   .   .   .   .

Hard has he toiled and richly earned his gains,
Ruined his fingers and spun out his brains
To acquire the right to ope his ponderous jaws,
As the great champion of Sedition's cause.
Once his soft words like streams of melted tar
Stuck in our ears and led us on to war;
But now we hear the self-same accents flow
Unmoved as quails when buried up in snow.
Is his voice weak? That dreadful voice, we're told,
Once made King George the Third through fear turn cold,
Europa's kingdoms to their centre shake,
When mighty Samuel bawl'd at Freedom's stake.

   .   .   .   .   .   .

Does his hand shake? When Sam cried out for war
His potent hand spread many a coat of tar,
That sinewy hand the feathers scattered o'er
Till Tories' jackets made their bellies sore.
Say, for whose sake has Time, that Barber gruff,
O'er his wise noddle shook his powder puff?
Was the task hard to hear the sage's noise?
Perhaps the awful sound had frightened boys;
But we, the sons of wisdom, fond to hear,
With joy had held the breath and oped the ear.
Did we e'en doubt that Solomon had spoke?
If so, has memory vanished into smoke."

The most of the succeeding numbers had reference to politics, but room was found for excursions in other fields : " Monier's Advertisement for a School," and " Newtonian Philosophy," served as pegs from which to hang rhymed jests, and the writers would very likely have taken a wider range if there had been a wider range in public interests. But politics dominated thought, and the wits were as bitter partisans as they were clever rhymesters. The poetry of the anti-Jacobin supplied them with the suggestion of form ; but there was not the lightness of touch or deft mimicry which characterized those remarkable political skits. As one reads the " Echo," and the " Green-house," and Trumbull's " McFingal," he is constantly reminded of the heaviness of the education which formed the substance of the writers' preparation for their task. The rudeness of the satire is the rudeness of a homespun society.

The authors of the " Echo," when the series came to be reissued in a volume, provided a somewhat solemn preface, in which they say : " The principal poems in this volume, under the title of the ' Echo,'

owed their origin to the accidental suggestion of a moment of literary sportiveness,
at a time when pedantry, affectation, and
bombast pervaded most of the pieces published in the gazettes, which were then the
principal vehicles of literary information.
Willing to lend their aid to check the progress of false taste in American literature,
the authors conceived that ridicule would
prove a powerful corrective, and that the
mode employed in the ' Echo' was the
best suited to this purpose. . . . But the
ridicule of a vitiated mode of writing was
not long the sole object of the 'Echo.'
The important political changes which soon
after occurred, not only in Europe, but in
America, produced a corresponding change
in the republic of letters ; and some of the
principal gazettes of this country exhibited
a disgusting display, not only of a perversion of taste in composition, but a still
greater perversion of principle, in that hid-
eous morality of revolutionary madness,
which, priding itself in an emancipation
from moral obligation, leveled the boundaries of virtue and vice, while it contemptuously derided the most amiable and sacred

feelings of our nature. Disgusted with the cruelties exhibited by the French Revolution at a very early stage of its progress, and viewing it as a consuming fire, which, in the course of its conflagration, threatened to destroy whatever was most valuable in society, the authors wished to contribute their efforts in stemming the torrents of Jacobinism in America, and resolved to render the ' Echo ' subservient to that purpose. They therefore proceeded to attack, as proper objects of satire, those tenets, as absurd in politics as pernicious in morals, the visionary scheme of equality, and the baleful doctrine that sanctions the pursuit of a good end by the most flagitious means."

Webster's judgment of the condition of literature in the country at a time when he was seeking to live by it is contained in a frank statement which he makes in one of his letters to Dr. Priestley. That philosopher had addressed certain letters to the inhabitants of Northumberland, in which he undertook to lecture them as a philosophical and wise Englishman might properly lecture the citizens of a young and inexperienced republic. Webster replied in ten

letters and a postscript, which were collected
into a pamphlet and published at New Haven, in 1800. He contends throughout that
Dr. Priestley did not know his countrymen,
and especially that he was ignorant of New
England; he corrects his political judgments, but admits the force in general of
his social and literary criticisms. The picture which Webster draws of the condition
of America at the beginning of the century
is instructive, and explains, indeed, much of
his own career : —

" I agree with you fully that our colleges
are disgracefully destitute of books and philosophical apparatus, and that a duty on
books without discrimination is highly im-
politic. Very many of the best authors
cannot be printed in the United States for
half a century or more ; and I am ashamed
to own that scarcely a branch of science
can be fully investigated in America for
want of books, especially original works.
This defect of our libraries I have experienced myself in searching for materials for
the history of Epidemic Diseases.

" In regard to the state of learning in
general, your remarks are not sufficiently

discriminating. You say there is 'less knowledge in America than in most of the countries of Europe.' The truth seems to be that in the Eastern States knowledge is more diffused among the laboring people than in any country on the globe. The learning of the people extends to a knowledge of their own tongue, of writing and arithmetic sufficient to keep their own simple accounts ; they read not only the Bible and newspapers, but almost all read the best English authors, as the 'Spectator,' 'Rambler,' and the works of Watts, Doddridge, and many others. If you can find any country in Europe where this is done to the same extent as in New England, I am very ill informed.

" But in the higher branches of literature our learning is superficial to a shameful degree. Perhaps I ought to except the science of law, which, being the road to political life, is probably as well understood as in Great Britain ; and ethics and political science have been greatly cultivated since the American Revolution. On political subjects I have no hesitation in saying that I believe the learning of our eminent statesmen to be superior to that of most European writers, and their opinions more correct. They have all the authors on these subjects, united with much experience, which no European country can have had. This has enabled our statesmen to correct many of the theories which lead astray European writers.

" But as to classical learning, history, civil and ecclesiastical, mathematics, astronomy, chymistry, botany, and natural history, excepting here and there a rare instance of a man who is eminent in some one of these branches, we may be said to have no learning at all, or a mere smattering. And what is more distressing to me, I see everywhere a disposition to decry the ancient and original authors, which I deem far superior to the modern, and from which the best modern writers have drawn the finest parts of their productions.

" There is another circumstance still more afflictive to a man who is attached, as I am, to a republican government, and one that I perceive has not occurred to you. This is that the equal distribution of estates and the small property of our citizens, both of which seem connected with our form of government, if not essential to it, actually tend to depress the sciences. Science demands leisure and money. Our citizens have property only to give their sons a four years' education, a time scarcely sufficient to give them a relish for learning, and far inadequate to wide and profound researches. As soon as a young man has closed this period of study, and while he is at the beginning of the alphabet of science, he must betake himself to a profession, he must hurry through a few books, — which, by the way, are rarely original works, but compilations and abridgments, — and then must enter upon practice, and get his living as well as he can. And as to libraries, we have no such things. There are not more than three or four tolerable libraries in America, and these are extremely imperfect. Great numbers of the most valuable authors have not found their way across the Atlantic.

" But if our young men had more time to read, their estates will not enable them to purchase the books requisite to make a learned man. And this inconvenience, resulting from our government and the state

of society, I know not how to remedy. As
this, however, is the government to which
you are attached, you will certainly do us a
great service if you can devise a plan for
avoiding its disadvantages. And I can further inform you that any application to legislatures for money will be unsuccessful.
The utmost we can do is to squeeze a little
money occasionally from the public treas-
uries to furnish buildings and a professor
or two. But as to libraries, public or private, men who do not understand their value
will be the last to furnish the means of procuring them. Besides, our rage for gain ab-
sorbs all other considerations; science is a
secondary object, and a man who has grown
suddenly from a dunghill, by a fortunate
throw of the die, avoids a man of learning
as you would a tiger. There are exceptions
to this remark, and some men of taste, here
and there scattered over our country, adorn
the sciences and the moral virtues. . . .

"If the Americans are yet in their leading-strings as to some parts of literature,
there is the more room for improvement;
and I am confident that the genius of my
fellow-citizens will not be slack in the im-

portant work.   You will please to recollect,
sir, that during one hundred and sixty years
of our childhood we were in our nonage;
respecting our parent and looking up to her
for books, science, and improvements. From
her we borrowed much learning and some
prejudices, which time alone can remove.
And be assured, Dr. Priestley, that the
parent is yet to derive some scientific improvements from the child.   Some false
theories, some errors in science, which the
British nation has imbibed from illustrious
men, and nourished from an implicit reliance on their authority, are to be prostrated
by the penetrating genius of America."

It is plain that Webster, aware of the deficiencies of his country in learning, was not
rendered entirely submissive by his knowledge, and was not at all disposed to accept
the relation of pupilage as a permanent one.
He worked with such material as he had,
and as a part of the intellectual movement
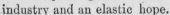
of the day brought for his contribution both
industry and an elastic hope.

CHAPTER IV.

POLITICAL WRITINGS.

WE have seen that a man who made a spelling-book could be a patriot in making it; it is easy to believe that a patriot in Webster's day could be a very active participant in public affairs. There was as yet no marked political class; every man of education was expected to write, talk, and act in politics, and Webster's temperament and education were certain to make him interested and active. He began very early to have a hand in those letters to newspapers which preceded the editorial article of the modern newspaper. The printer of a newspaper was substantially its editor, and was likely to be a man engaged in public affairs, but his paper was less the medium for his own views than a convenient vehicle for carrying the opinions and arguments of lawyers, ministers, and others.

Webster began contributing to the " Con-

necticut Courant," published in Hartford,
as early as 1780, his first contribution being
some remarks on Benedict Arnold's letter of
October 7th to the inhabitants of America.
He wrote again the next week on Arnold's
treason, and for the next four or five years
was an occasional contributor upon subjects
of finance, banking, the pay of soldiers, con-
gressional action, events of the war, and
copyright. "In 1783," he writes of himself, "the discontents in Connecticut, ex-
cited by an opposition to the grant of five
years' extra pay to the officers of the army,
became alarming, and two thirds of the
towns sent delegates to a convention in Mid-
dletown to devise measures to prevent the
resolve of Congress from being carried into
execution. I then commenced my career
as a political writer, devoting weeks and
months to support the resolves of Congress.
. . . Of the discontents in Connecticut in
1783, which threatened a commotion, there
is no account in any of the histories of the
United States, — not even in Marshall's, —
except a brief account in my history; the
present generation being entirely ignorant
of the events. The history of this whole

period, from the peace of 1783 to the adoption of the Constitution, is, in all the histories for schools, except mine, a barren, imperfect account; although it was a period of great anxiety, when it was doubtful whether anarchy or civil war was to be our fate." [1]

This was written in 1838, when Webster was eighty years old. The character of that interregnum of 1783–1789 is more generally recognized now; and it is interesting to see how an old man, recalling his earliest entrance into public life, emphasizes the service which he rendered upon the side of good government. By early associations, and by the predilections of a mind which inherited a large share of Anglo-Saxon political sense, Webster was from the first a Federalist in politics. In 1785 he published a pamphlet entitled "Sketches of American Policy," which he always claimed was the first public plea for a government to take the place of the Confederation, under which the war had been carried on. He held a correspondence with Mr. Madison, in 1805,

[1] Letter to L. Gaylord Clark, *Lippincott's Magazine,* April, 1870.

for the purpose of substantiating this claim, since it had recently been asserted that the federal government sprang from Hamilton's thought. Mr. Madison very temperately and sensibly wrote to Webster : —

" The change in our government, like most other important improvements, ought to be ascribed rather to a series of causes than to any particular and sudden one, and to the participation of many rather than to the efforts of a single agent. It is certain that the general idea of revising and enlarging the scope of the federal authority, so as to answer the necessary purposes of the Union, grew up in many minds, and by natural degrees, during the experienced inefficacy of the old Confederation. The discernment of General Hamilton must have rendered him an early patron of the idea. That the public attention was called to it by yourself at an early period is well known."

We are not especially concerned with Webster's claim except as it illustrates his character and activity. He was a busybody, if I may recover to better uses a somewhat ignoble word. We have seen

busy body

him traveling back and forth, visiting the
state capitals and public men in behalf of
his " Grammatical Institute," lecturing and
writing, projecting magazines, and putting
himself into the midst of whatever was going on. The air was full of political talk,
and Webster was the conductor that drew
off some of it. He rushed eagerly into
pamphlet-writing, both because he had something to say, and because he never stepped
back to see if any one else was about to say
it. He had no public character to preserve,
and he issued his pamphlet as he delivered
his sentiments upon many subjects, — to
whomever he might catch. He carried it
to Mount Vernon and put it into the hands
of General Washington, and Madison saw
it there. The nickname of the Monarch,
which Belknap and Hazard gave him, fitted
a young man of aggressive self-confidence,
who saw no reason why he should not have
his say upon the subject which was upper-
most in men's minds, and used the means
most natural to him and most convenient.

Alexander Hamilton was but a year older
than Noah Webster, and was indeed a much
younger man when he first took part in the

discussion of public affairs. Hamilton was a man with a genius for statesmanship ; in Webster we see very significantly marks of political common sense, the presence of which in the American mind at that day made Hamilton's leadership possible. It would be hard to find a better illustration of the average political education of Americans of the time than is shown by Webster in this pamphlet and in other of his writings. We are accustomed sometimes to speak of the Constitution as a half-miraculous gift to the American people, and to look with exceptional reverence upon the framers of that instrument. Well, that mind is on the whole quite as sound as the contemptuous tone taken .by Von Holst when he affirms that "the Constitution had been extorted from the grinding necessity of a reluctant people." [1] In these words, however, Von Holst himself scarcely does justice to his own convictions, and they are rather an extreme form of protest against an extravagant adulation of the Constitution. Better instruments on paper have been drawn and applied to conditions of

[1] *Constitutional History of the United States,* i. 63.

society which were fatal to their efficacy;
but the calling of the convention, the fram-
ing of the Constitution, and the final adoption were possible because in the community at large the ideas of freedom and of
self-government had already been formu-
lated in local institutions for generations,
and for generations had been moulding the
character of the popular thought. The
towns, the parishes, the boroughs, of the
early colonies were the inheritors of commu-
nal ideas which had filtered from Germanic
free communities through English parishes;
under the favoring conditions of a new
world and its unchecked enterprise they
had become political units of great integrity.
The colonies, with their local government,
modified rather than controlled by royal or
proprietary influence, had already learned
many lessons of autonomy: the period of
the war had confirmed these several powers,
and the conclusion of the war found them
still in possession of their interior organic
life, and lacking only that sovereignty which
they had resisted and overthrown. But the
state life was incomplete: there was an absence of a solid sovereignty in which the

States could rest, and the political thought of the independent colonies required for its final fulfillment the depositary of national consciousness which the King and Parliament had been, but could no longer be. It was the working out of this practical political thought which issued in the Constitution and central government, and it was possible to be worked out only because there had been generations of Americans trained in political life.

Webster was one of these men. He was the product of the forces which had been at work in the country from the earliest days. English freedom, which had forced its ways to these shores, had grown and increased under the fostering care of self-government and native industry. He had been born and brought up in a New England country village, the type of the freest and most determinate local government ; he had been educated at a democratic college ; he had shouldered his musket in a war for the defense not of his State alone, but of his country, vague and ill defined though its organic form might be. When, therefore, the war was over, and the country was free and compelled to manage its own affairs, he was qualified to take part in that management, and his temper led him to look for fundamental grounds of conduct.

His " Sketches of American Policy " thus interests us as the political thinking of a young American, of lively disposition, candid mind, and rash confidence. It could not help being a reflection of other literature and thought; but its best character is in its sturdy and resolute assertion of English freedom as requiring a central authority in which to rest. It is curious, in the opening pages, to see how, in his theories of government, he is led away by the popular and alluring philosophy of Rousseau and Rousseau's interpreter, Jefferson. When he undertakes to explain the rationale of government he is a young man, captivated by the current mode ; when he reaches the immediate, practical duty he is an Englishman, speaking to the point, and lighting upon the one unanswerable demand of American political life at the time. In the earlier pages of his " Sketches " he lays down his Theory of Government, which is, in brief, that of the *contrat social*, but presented in

a homely form, which brings it nearer to the
actual life of men ; he concludes his observation with a definition of the most perfect
practicable system of government as "a
government where the right of *making* laws
is vested in the greatest number of individuals, and the power of *executing* them in
the smallest number." "In large communities," he adds, "the individuals are too
numerous to assemble for the purpose of
legislation : for which reason, the people
appear by substitutes or agents, — persons
of their own choice. A representative democracy seems, therefore, to be the most
perfect system of government that is practicable on earth." He finds no such government on the Continent of Europe, or in
history ; but when he comes to America he
views with satisfaction a state of things
which renders possible the actual fulfillment
of his ideal. "America, just beginning to
exist, has the science and the experience of
all nations to direct her in forming plans of
government." There is an equal distribution of landed property, freed from the laws
of entail and primogeniture ; there is no
standing army, and there is freedom from

ecclesiastical tyranny; education is general; there is no artificial rank in society, and from necessity Americans are not confined to single lines of industry; but various occupations will meet in one man. "Knowledge is diffused and genius roused by the very situation of America."

From these considerations he proceeds to lay down a "Plan of Policy for improving the Advantages and perpetuating the Union of the American States." This union, he shows, cannot depend upon a standing army, upon ecclesiastical authority, or upon the fear of an external force; it must find its reason in the constitutions of the States, and he sees, therefore, the need of a supreme head, in which the power of all the States is united. "There must be a supreme head, clothed with the same power to make and enforce laws respecting the general policy of all the States, as the legislatures of the respective States have to make laws binding on those States respecting their own internal police. The truth of this is taught by the principles of government, and confirmed by the experience of America. Without such a head the States cannot be *united*, and all attempts to conduct the measures of the continent will prove but governmental farces. So long as any individual State has power to defeat the measures of the other twelve, our pretended union is but a name, and our confederation a cobweb." He illustrates his point by the analogy of the Constitution of Connecticut. It is clear that by the head of the Union he meant the combined executive and legislative force, which in the Constitution was vested in the President and Congress. He recognizes the necessity of an authoritative head, but he had not in his own mind separated the powers of government. He clings fast to the doctrine that all power is vested in the people, and proceeds from the people, and he pleads for such a union as may be analogous to the union of towns in the State, where the power of all the towns united is compulsory over the conduct of a single member. "The general concerns of the continent may be reduced to a few heads; but in all the affairs that respect the whole, Congress must have the same power to enact laws and compel obedience throughout the continent as the legislatures

of the several States have in their respective jurisdictions. If Congress have any
power, they must have the whole power of
the continent. Such a power would not
abridge the sovereignty of each State in
any article relating to its own government.
The internal police of each State would be
still under the sole superintendence of its
legislature. But in a matter that equally
respects all the States no individual State
has more than a thirteenth part of the legislative authority, and consequently has no
right to decide what measure shall or shall
not take place on the continent. A majority of the States *must* decide; our confederation cannot be permanent unless founded
on that principle; nay, more, the States cannot be said to be *united* till such a principle
is adopted in its utmost latitude. If a single town or precinct could counteract the
will of a whole State, would there be any
government in that State? It is an established principle in government that the will
of the minority must submit to that of the
majority; and a single State or a minority
of States ought to be disabled to resist the
will of the majority, as much as a town or

county in any State is disabled to prevent the execution of a statute law of the legislature. It is on this principle, and *this alone*, that a free State can be governed; it is on this principle alone that the American States can exist as a confederacy of republics. Either the several States must continue separate, totally independent of each other, and liable to all the evils of jealousy, dispute, and civil dissension, — nay, liable to a civil war, upon any clashing of interests, — or they must constitute a general head, composed of representatives from all the States, and vested with the power of the whole continent to enforce their decisions. There is no other alternative. One of these events must inevitably take place, and the revolution of a few years will verify the prediction."

In answering possible objections to the scheme, he rests in the power of the people, who " forever keep the sole right of legislation in their own representatives, but divest themselves wholly of any right to the administration." He refuses to believe that there is any danger from centralization so long as the people use the power which is

vested in them. " These things," he concludes, "demand our early and careful attention : a general diffusion of knowledge ;
the encouragement of industry, frugality,
and virtue ; and a sovereign power at the
head of the States. *All* are essential to our
peace and prosperity, but on an energetic
continental government principally depend
our tranquillity at home and our respecta-
bility among foreign nations. We ought to
generalize [that is, delocalize] our ideas and
our measures. We ought not to consider
ourselves as inhabitants of a particular State
only, but as *Americans*, as the common subjects of a great empire. We cannot and
ought not wholly to divest ourselves of provincial views and attachments, but we should
subordinate them to the general interests of
the continent. As a member of a family
every individual has some domestic interests ; as a member of a corporation he has
other interests ; as an inhabitant of a State
he has a more extensive interest ; as a citizen and subject of the American empire he
has a national interest far superior to all
others. Every relation in society constitutes
some obligations, which are proportional to

the magnitude of the society. A good prince does not ask what will be for the interest of a county or small district in his dominions, but what will promote the prosperity of his kingdom. In the same manner, the citizens of this New World should inquire, not what will aggrandize this town or that State, but what will augment the power, secure the tranquillity, multiply the subjects, and advance the opulence, the dignity, and the virtues, of the United States. Self-interest, both in morals and politics, is and ought to be the ruling principle of mankind ; but this principle must operate in perfect conformity to social and political obligations. Narrow views and illiberal prejudices may for a time produce a selfish system of politics in each State; but a few years' experience will correct our ideas of self-interest, and convince us that a selfishness which excludes others from a participation of benefits is, in all cases, self-ruin, and that *provincial* interest is inseparable from *national interest.*"

It will be seen that Webster, though confused sometimes in his phraseology, and weak in his philosophy, did see with an

English freeman's political instinct the practical bearings of his subject, and in his
broad, comprehensive survey disclosed that
large American apprehension of freedom
and nationality which underlay the best
thought of his time. His pamphlet is not
a piece of elegant writing, and it is introduced by superficial theorizing ; but the
practical value is great. Thoughts which
have so entered into our political consciousness as to be trite and commonplace are
presented as the new possession of a young
man lately from college, and it is fair to
judge of the current speculation of his time
by the results here gathered into logical
order. Webster, as I said before, may be
taken in this pamphlet as an admirable example of the American political thinker,
who has worked out, under the new conditions of this continent, ideas and principles
which his ancestors brought from England.
He thinks he has invented something new,
but the worth of his thought is in its experience. In a period when every one was
engaged in rearranging the universe upon
some improved plan of his own, it is not
surprising that those who thought they had

a brand-new nation on their hands should
have made a serious business of nationaliz-
ing themselves. They thought they were
starting afresh from a purely philosophical
basis, and they were greatly concerned about
their premises; as a matter of fact, their
premises were often highly artificial, while
their conclusions were sound, for these really
drew their life from the historic development
of free institutions, and the nation which was
formally instituted had long had an organic
process. Webster himself, twenty years
after, when referring to this pamphlet, had
the good sense to say, "The remarks in the
first three sketches are general, and some of
them I now believe to be too visionary for
practice; but the fourth sketch was intended
expressly to urge, by all possible arguments,
the necessity of a radical alteration in our
system of general government, and an outline is there suggested." He adds, "As a
private man, young and unknown, I could
do but little; but that little I did."

In the autumn of 1786 he went to Philadelphia at the invitation of Franklin, and
stayed there a year. He maintained himself in part by teaching, being master of an

Episcopal academy ; but his interest centred upon the debates of the Constitutional Convention, then in session, and a month after it rose he published " An Examination of the Leading Principles of the Federal Constitution," which was, in effect, a popular defense of the work of the Convention, especially as regards the division of the legislature into two houses. The paper shows rather zeal and fervor than acuteness, and seems to have been hastily written to serve some special and temporary purpose. It has a magniloquence not elsewhere found in his writings, as when he says : " This western world now beholds an æra important beyond conception, and which posterity will number with the age of the Czar of Muscovy, and with the promulgation of the Jewish laws at Mount Sinai. The names of those men who have digested a system of constitutions for the American empire will be enrolled with those of Zamolxis and Odin, and celebrated by posterity with the honors which less enlightened nations have paid to the fabled demi-gods of antiquity. . . . In the formation of our Constitution the wisdom of all ages is collected ; the legislators of antiquity are consulted, as well as the opinions and interests of the millions who are concerned. In short, it is an empire of reason." In all this there is a flurry of enthusiasm which was not confined to Webster.

Later still, in 1793, he was placed in a more responsible position, as editor of a new daily newspaper in New York. He had been writing under the signature of Candor in the "Courant" upon the French Revolution, taking a somewhat Gallican position, when he chanced to meet Genet at dinner in New York. Conversation with that gentleman caused a change in his views, and it was during this visit to New York that Mr. James Watson proposed to him to establish a newspaper there in the defense of Washington's administration. With his ardent attachment to Washington, and his adhesion generally to the federal party, he accepted the invitation, and established the " American Minerva," which subsequently became the " New York Commercial Advertiser." In conducting the paper he introduced an economical device, which was novel at the time, but has since become an

established mode with daily newspapers :
he issued a semi-weekly paper, called the
" Herald," which was made up from the
columns of the daily " Minerva " without
recomposition of type.

The political situation which led to the
establishment of the " Minerva " was that
created by the intrigues of Citizen Genet,
and by the bitter hostility to Washington's
administration on the part of the French
sympathizers. Washington had issued his
proclamation of neutrality, and the Jacobin
clubs had opened upon him with their newspapers and pamphlets and public addresses
in the most virulent manner. It is scarcely
too much to say that the animosity between
the French and anti-French parties in the
United States was keener — it certainly was
madder — than that which had existed between Americans and Englishmen during
the war which had so lately closed. The
earlier movements of the French Revolution had called out in America even more
than in England the liveliest expectations
of a golden age. Americans, flattered by
the French alliance and by the reputation
in which their young republic was held,

were intoxicated with vanity, and filled also with an eager hope that principles of which they were standard-bearers were to be dominant in Europe. The theoretical and *doctrinaire* views which seemed for the time to be justified by the success of the American people came to stand for universal principles of reason, capable of bearing all the weight of human experience, and of serving in the place of religion. The most enthusiastic, beholding a new era, were only a few steps in advance of more cautious men, and the new *régime* in France received the sympathy not only of Jefferson and Madison, but of Washington and Hamilton. It was only when the flood-gates were opened that the uniform sentiment was broken in upon, and parties were formed of "Gallomaniacs" on one side, as their enemies called them, and anti-Gallicans on the other. But this split into two parties had occurred before Genet arrived, and the breach was only widened by that headstrong minister's action. There can be little doubt that the prudence of Washington, aided by the conservative Hamilton and the unwilling Jefferson, saved the country at the time from committing itself to the insanity of active coöperation with the raging French republic.

The support of the administration was to be looked for not only in legislatures, but in the public press, which was rapidly becoming a power in the country. Certainly the flames of passion and prejudice were fanned most persistently by such journalists as Freneau and Bache on one side, and Cobbett on the other, and it was evident that the war over the question was to be fought largely in the columns of newspapers. Webster's federalism was staunch, so was his personal loyalty to Washington; but I think he was asked to manage the new paper chiefly because in his writings thus far, both upon political and general topics, he had shown himself to have that direct and homely style which makes itself understood by the people because it is in the dialect of the people. At any rate, he began at once vigorously to write and print articles bearing upon the great question of the day. He informed himself of the historical process of the French Revolution, but whatever he wrote was in reference to the effect upon

the United States. Webster's patriotism was
the best education for a true regard of public affairs in France. His instinct for unity,
his conception of the future of the United
States, his unbounded faith in American
ideas, all served to make him fight any proposal which would complicate the United
States with foreign powers.

His hand is seen in various parts of the
paper for the five years during which he
was connected with it. The French Revolution and all the complications growing
out of it were treated with steadfast reference to the interests of the United States,
and blows were dealt unceasingly upon the
democratic party, as the anti-Federalists
were beginning to call themselves. Webster digested the foreign news, wrote articles and paragraphs, and used the machinery
which belonged to a paper of that day. It
is not unlikely that he wrote letters to himself ; it is certain that he wrote a series of
essays entitled " The Times," pithy, forcible
homilies and comments, expressed generally
in a colloquial form, and intended, evidently,
to be driven home sharply and positively.
I give an extract from one as indicating

something of the manner of these *conciones ad populum*: —

. . . "Our government is a government of universal toleration. The freedom of America, its greatest blessing, secures to every citizen the right of thinking, of speaking, of worshiping and acting as he pleases, provided he does not violate the laws. The only people in America who have dared to violate this freedom are the democratical incendiaries, who have proceeded to threaten violence to tories and aristocrats and federal republicans; that is, to people not of their party. Every threat of this kind is an act of tyranny; an attempt to abridge the rights of a fellow-citizen. If a man is persecuted for his opinions, it is wholly immaterial whether the persecution springs from one man or from a society of the people, — when men are disposed to persecute. Power is always right; weakness always wrong. Power is always insolent and despotic: whether exercised in throwing its opposers into a bastile; burning them at the stake; torturing them on a rack; beheading them with a guillotine; or taking them off, as at the massacre of St. Bartholomew, at a general sweep. Power is the same in Turkey as in America. When the will of man is raised above law, it is always tyranny and despotism, whether it is the will of a bashaw or of bastard patriots."

The articles which Webster contributed in reviewing the historical movement of the French Revolution were worked over into a pamphlet, which he published in 1794. There were other questions belonging to this time which grew out of the relations between the young republic and European nations. In running over the files of the "Minerva," one is struck with the predominating influence of Europe in American affairs. Every change which took place abroad was watched with reference to its influence on home politics. The habit of regarding America as dependent upon Europe, which underlay so much of the thought of the time, was not easily laid aside, and the tests applied to the conduct of American affairs were of European precedents. The secretary of state was then and long after the leading man of the Cabinet. It is indeed only lately that his comparative importance has been lessened, and that of the secretaries of the treasury and of the interior increased.

Webster's pen was employed on the great questions which arose on the rights of neutral nations, and especially on the policy contained in Jay's Treaty. In vindication of this treaty he published a series of papers, under the signature of Curtius, twelve in all, but the sixth and seventh were contributed by James Kent, afterward Chancellor Kent. The papers came out at the same time with the series signed Camillus, written by Hamilton and King.[1] When the first number of Curtius appeared, Jefferson wrote of it to Madison: " I send you by post one of the pieces, Curtius, lest it should not have come to you otherwise. It is evidently written by Hamilton, giving a first and general view of the subject, that the public mind might be kept a little in check, till he could resume the subject more at large from the beginning, under his second signature, Camillus. . . . I gave a copy or two, by way of experiment, to

[1] The statement that King assisted Hamilton is made by H. C. Lodge, in *The Life and Letters of George Cabot*, p. 84.

honest-hearted men of common understanding, and they were not able to parry the
sophistry of Curtius. I have ceased, therefore, to give them. Hamilton is really a
colossus to the anti-republican party. . . .
For God's sake, take up your pen, and give
a fundamental reply to Curtius and Camillus." But Madison did not yield to Jefferson's entreaty. In these papers Webster
reviewed the treaty article by article, and
kept closely to his text, in the last number
only enlarging upon the insidious character of much of the opposition to the treaty,
as connected with the machinations of the
French party. It was not without reason
that Mr. King expressed the opinion to Mr.
Jay "that the essays of Curtius had contributed more than any other papers of the
same kind to allay the discontent and opposition to the treaty;" assigning as a reason that they were peculiarly well adapted
to the understanding of the people at large.

Webster had the newspaper faculty, and
was as omniscient as any editor need be.
A consideration of his general labors be-
longs elsewhere, but it ought to be noted
here that he was prompt to see the perils

which underlay American slavery. He discussed the subject, indeed, chiefly in its industrial relations, but he regarded these as
affecting parties and national well-being.
As early as 1793 he delivered an address
before the Connecticut Society for the Pro-
motion of Freedom " On the Effects of Slavery on Morals and Industry," and shortly
afterward expanded the address into a treatise. His work bristles with historical illustrations, for it was the habit then more
than later to draw inferences from foreign
facts ; there had not yet accumulated that
great swelling volume of home testimony
which made reference to experience outside
of America unnecessary and rather imper-
tinent. His remedy for the existing evil is
the elevation of slaves to the rank of ten-
ants, not in a sudden emancipation, but in
the gradual selection of the most capable,
and he finds his most satisfactory example
in the experiment made thirty years before
by the Chancellor of Poland. The appeal
is not greatly to the conscience, but to the
interest of men. He sums up the argument
at the close with the words : " The industry, the commerce, and the moral char-

acter of the United States will be immensely benefited by the change. Justice and Humanity require it; Christianity *commands* it." He had not long been conducting the " Minerva " before he took up the subject again, reminding the public of this treatise. " In that pamphlet," he says, " I endeavored to show by arguments and facts that the labor of slaves is less productive than that of freemen. A doctrine of this kind, if clearly and incontrovertibly established, will perhaps go farther in abolishing the practice of enslaving men than any declamation on the immorality and cruelty of the practice." He then takes up the statistics which had accumulated since the publication of his pamphlet, showing in a forcible manner that the Northern Free States were steadily gaining on the Southern Slave States, and carries forward the argument with great acuteness. " What," he asks, " has produced this difference in the productiveness of the labor in the Northern division ? Peace and good markets have been common to both divisions; and the laboring people in the Northern States were as free before the year 1791 as since.

What, then, has stimulated the industry of the free laborers since that period? The answer is obvious. An augmentation of capital operating upon their free labor. It is probable there has been an augmentation of capital throughout the United States, though I am convinced that augmentation has been much greater in the Northern than in the Southern. But my general remark is that an increase of capital must be felt by the laboring people themselves to produce its full effect in stimulating industry. The benefits of capital and good markets in the Northern States are experienced by the men who labor; in the Southern States this is not the case among the slaves, who make a great proportion among the laborers. It is of little consequence to a slave whether his master employs in business ten thousand or one thousand, or whether he gets four dollars or two for a hundred of tobacco. In both cases he plods on at his task with the same slow, reluctant pace. A *freeman*, on the other hand, labors with double diligence when he gets a high price for his produce; and this I apprehend to be a principal cause which has in the last two years occasioned such a surprising difference of exports in favor of the Northern States."

Webster's connection with the " Minerva " continued for about five years, when he abandoned it as unprofitable; but his industry may be inferred from the fact that his writings upon the paper, inclusive of translations from foreign languages, would amount to twenty octavo volumes.

His withdrawal from the conduct of a daily newspaper did not mean his indifference to public affairs. Near the close of his stay in New York he wrote "A Letter on the Value and Importance of the American Commerce to Great Britain, addressed to a Gentleman of Distinction in London." His aim was to emphasize the judgment that the commercial interests of the two countries were closely interwoven, and that in the complication of European politics the United States, if compelled to make any alliance, was most naturally related to England. In 1802 he published his laborious and learned "Essay on the Rights of Neutral Nations," in which he took a position at variance on a single point with that which he held when vindicating Jay's Treaty a few years before. In that treaty Great Britain had stipulated that naval stores should be prohibited as contraband of war, and Webster, in common with others, assumed with reluctance that such prohibition was in accordance with the general law of nations, although admitting that this was the most vulnerable article of the treaty. Further investigation satisfied him of his error, and he frankly avowed it in the later essay, where he says: " For the honor of my country, and the essential interests of her commerce, I regret that the administration, in the very commencement of the national government, has consented to abandon ground which the nations of Europe had, for more than a century, been struggling to obtain and to fortify. I have no hesitation in declaring that no considerations of public danger can justify a commercial nation in consenting to enlarge the field of contraband ; nor can there be an apology for the renewal of the clause in the compact, by which our true interests and essential rights have been surrendered." Following the maxim that "Free ships make free goods," he estab-

lishes himself on the proposition that
" neutrals have a better right to trade than
nations have to fight and plunder." Webster argued strenuously in maintenance of
rights which were in jeopardy, and the
disregard of which by Great Britain had
much to do with the War of 1812–1814.
He was writing at the beginning of Jefferson's first administration, with all the dis-
trust which the federalist party felt of the
President's foreign policy, but it cannot be
said that his examination of the subject is
other than fair and impartial.

How bitterly he could write as a partisan is shown by the long "Address to the
President of the United States on the subject of his Address," published in 1802, and
called out by Jefferson's inaugural, then six
months old. The principles laid down in
that address, in the midst of much fine
rhetoric, had begun to be shown in practice,
and Webster employs argument and invec-
tive to lay bare the falseness of Jefferson's
professions. His longest and sharpest attack
is upon the policy pursued by the President
in rewarding his followers with office, — a
policy in accord with the principles laid

down in the inaugural. We are accustomed nowadays to strong statements of the viciousness of the spoils system, but no advocate of civil service reform has attacked the full-grown system of party rewards with any more vigor than Webster showed at the beginning of the system. " No, sir!" he exclaims indignantly, " no individual or party has a *claim* or *right* to any office whatever; " and he shows with exceeding clearness the tendency of such a doctrine. In his subsequent occasional addresses one finds frequently the note of alarm here struck. Webster was a fervid Federalist, and the accession of the democratic party to power was a shock to his confidence in the perpetuity of the Union from which he never wholly recovered. When the election for President occurred in 1832, and it was clear that Jackson would be returned, Webster refused to go to the polls ; he sent away the carriage which came for him. Of what use was it to vote? But the next year, when his son-in-law, Judge Ellsworth, was a candidate for the governor's place, his faith revived a little, and he found it possible to vote.

Webster's federalism had one significant expression in the preliminary measures which led to the Hartford Convention. In January, 1814, Judge Joseph Lyman, of Northampton, wrote to him at Amherst, where he was then living, and proposed a meeting of the most discreet and intelligent inhabitants of the county of Hampshire, for the purpose of a free and dispassionate discussion respecting public concerns. A meeting was held in Northampton, January 19th, at which Webster proposed that the several towns in the vicinity should call a convention of delegates from the legislatures of the Northern States, to agree upon and urge certain amendments to the Constitution for the restoration of the equilibrium between the North and the South. He and two others were appointed to draft a circular letter, and this circular, written by Webster, was sent out under Judge Lyman's name. In consequence of the appeal, a number of towns sent petitions to the General Court of Massachusetts asking for such a convention. It was not judged expedient to call one at that session; but in October of the same year Harrison Gray Otis reintroduced the measure, and Mr. Webster, then a member of the legislature, supported it in a speech. The Hartford Convention thereupon was called, and while Mr. Webster was not a member of it, he was so far involved in its organization that he afterward published a sketch of these earlier steps, though he did not there state in full his own intimate connection with the movement.

Webster's federalism was something more than a partisan sentiment. In following his political thought, it is easily perceived that his creed of party was subordinate to his larger belief in the American Republic. His writings upon public affairs, which are very considerable, constantly reveal this dominant thought. The very vagaries — which, as we have seen, and shall see again, rendered some of his ideas amusing and vainglorious — were but the disorderly and ill-regulated whims of a sincere patriotism. Americanism in literature and language may become fantastic, but in politics there is pretty sure to be room for the most ardent love of country to expand itself without becoming a bubble, and it is certain that Web-

ster's political writings were marked by a
largeness of conception and a clear understanding of national lines which redeem
them from insignificance. They had their
influence upon his contemporaries, yet they
were, after all, ephemeral. Had he concentrated his powers upon political themes, it
is not impossible that he should have been
a journalist, for instance, of influence and
even celebrity. But there was a weakness
on this side. He did not bring to the discussion of great public questions that weight
of learning and breadth of argument which
will sustain political writings when the
immediate occasion has passed. Whether
writing pamphlets or newspaper articles,
he was essentially a writer of the day, of
importance in pressing home arguments
calling for immediate results, but lacking
the art of literature and the commanding
thought of a statesman. He had a true sentiment in politics, and he was able also to
see practical issues clearly; but his mind was
analytical rather than constructive, and his
restlessness of life was indicative of a certain instability of temper which kept him
uneasily employed about many things rather

than steadfast and single-minded. It would
be too much to say that he failed as a political writer, and fell back on his philological
and school-master studies ; yet it is very
likely that, in the various excursions which
he made into politics and general literature,
he discovered by successive trials that there
was one pursuit more than all which really
belonged to him, and the constancy with
which he followed it is in singular contrast
with the multitudinous experiments which
seemed to occupy the period of his life
between 1785 and 1802.

CHAPTER V.

EXCURSIONS.

In one of his political papers Webster sketches the average American of his time: "He makes a variety of utensils, — rough, indeed, but such as will answer his purpose; he is a husbandman in summer and a mechanic in winter; he travels about the country; he converses with a variety of professions; he reads public papers; he has access to a parish library, and thus becomes acquainted with history and politics, and every man in New England is a theologian." I have already intimated that Webster dissipated his strength, and it is only fair to state the facts in the light of the conditions under which he lived. In the unorganized and fluent state of society there was little room for a specialist; or, to change the phrase for a more exact one, there was too much room. Every educated man was called upon to occupy himself with a great variety of tasks.

The demand made by the republican experiment was very great. People had practiced local self-government under monarchical supervision for a long time; now they were bound to extend the sphere of their political activity, and in the adjustment of the new machinery there was abundant opportunity for all the ingenuity and wit of the educated class to exercise itself. Then there was a great impetus given by politics to the democratizing of the nation, and, in the rapid social changes of the day, the educated class found itself well shaken up with the mechanic. The terms which Webster employs of the average American may easily be applied to all classes. Nice distinctions of rank and occupation could not easily be maintained in a country where there was vastly more land than could be tilled, where enterprise of every kind was limited only by lack of labor, and where every citizen had his hand on the wheels of government.

In a conventional way Webster would be classed amongst the educated men of the country: he had received his diploma at one of the chief colleges; his occupations were intellectual; his profession was the liberal

one of the law.   Yet in a more real way he
was a farmer's son, and though he ceased
early from manual labor his mental affilia-
tions were with the plain people rather than
with the intellectual ones. He seized all
subjects by their practical side, and his instinct was to apply the rough-and-ready
rules of common sense to all questions,
whether of politics, theology, or philology.
Such men as Belknap and Hazard looked
with disdain upon him ; they felt rather than
said that Webster was not one of them. So,
when living in Hartford, Webster was not
identified with the circle of Hartford wits.
His mind was not subtle or graceful ; he
had not the faculty of creating, nor, so far
as I can discover, of appreciating literature ;
but he had an uncommonly active manu-
facturing mind, and in his intellectual work-
shop he made, as he said of his average
American, " a variety of utensils, — rough,
indeed, but such as will answer his purpose."

He had much in common with Franklin,
to whom he was strongly drawn. He had
Franklin's eminent common sense and home-
liness, by which he gained a hearing from
plain men and women ; but he had not

Franklin's crystal style, his instinct for the fewest and best words, his happy use of a language which seemed made for his thoughts. We noticed that in the spelling-book he displayed a fondness for the wisdom of proverbs and familiar sayings, and among his earliest writings were a series of pithy homilies to the people upon questions of morals and manners, published first in the Connecticut "Courant," but early collected into a volume entitled "The Prompter;" a little book which one may trace to a good many different printing-offices and to various sections of the country, certainly the most widely spread of Webster's writings, after his text-books, and the most worthy of a repeated life. If I am not mistaken, it is even now making its little mark on character.

The sub-title of the book is "A Commentary on Common Sayings and Subjects, which are full of Common Sense, — the best sense in the world;" and in the preface, explanatory of the purpose of the book, Webster's manner as a popular writer is well shown. "A Prompter," he remarks of the happy title, "is the man who, in plays, sits behind the scenes, looks over the rehearser, and with a moderate voice corrects him when wrong, or assists his recollection when he forgets the next sentence. A Prompter, then, says but little, but that little is very necessary, and often does much good. He helps the actors on the stage at a dead lift, and enables them to go forward with spirit and propriety. The writer of this little book took it into his head to prompt the numerous actors upon the great theatre of life; and he sincerely believes that his only motive was to do good. He cast about to find the method of writing calculated to do the most general good. He wanted to whip vice and folly out of the country; he thought of 'Hudibras' and 'McFingal,' and pondered well whether he should attempt the masterly style of those writings. He found this would not do, for, like most modern rhymers, he is no poet, and he always makes bungling work at imitation.

" The Prompter thought of the grave diction of sober, moral writers, and the pompous, flowing style of modern historians. Fame began now to prick up his vanity to try an imitation of the great Dr. Robertson, Dr. Johnson, and Mr. Gibbon, those giants of literature. He thought if he could muster dollars enough to buy a style-mill, which those heroes of science undoubtedly used to cut out sentences for their works, he should succeed to a tittle. But then it occurred to him that when he had cut and shaped his periods into exact squares, diamonds, pentagons, parallelograms, and other mathematical figures, they might not contain very clear, precise, definite ideas ; one half of his readers would not understand him. The style-mill, then, or, as some people contemptuously call it, the word-mill, would not answer the Prompter's purpose of doing as much good as possible by making men wiser and better.

" At length he determined to have nothing to do with a brilliant flow of words, a pompous elegance of diction ; for what has the world to do with the sound of words ? The Prompter's business is with the world at large, and the mass of mankind are concerned only with common things. A dish of high-seasoned turtle is rarely found ; it sometimes occurs at a gentleman's table, and then the chance is it produces a surfeit. But good solid roast beef is a common dish for all men ; it sits easy on the stomach, it supports, it strengthens and invigorates. Vulgar sayings and proverbs, so much despised by the literary epicures, the Chesterfields of the age, are the roast beef of science. They contain the experience, the wisdom, of nations and ages compressed into the compass of a nutshell. To crack the shell and extract the contents to feed those who have appetites is the aim of this little book."

The several essays are expansive of the familiar sayings or proverbs which stand for their titles, as, "It will do for the present," "I told you so," "He is sowing his wild oats," "He would have his own way," "A stitch in time saves nine," "Any other time will do as well," "He has come out at the little end of the horn." The papers are all short, and no time is wasted in coming at the point ; indeed, there is a succession of thrusts in each paper, and the reader is prodded more or less efficiently at each step. Here, to give a single example, is Number XVIII.: "What is everybody's business is nobody's."

"The consequence is that everybody and

nobody are just the same thing, — a truth
most pointedly exemplified in the kitchen
of a Southern nabob. 'Phil!' says the mistress, with the air of an empress. Phil appears. 'Go tell Peg to tell Sue to come
along here and pick up a needle.' 'Yes,
ma'am,' answers Phil, and waddles back
like a duck. 'Peg, mistress says you must
tell Sue to go to her and pick up a needle.'
Peg carries the message to Sue, but Sue is
busy cleaning a candlestick. 'Well,' says
Sue, 'I will go as soon as I have done.'
The mistress wants the needle; she waits
ten or fifteen minutes, grows impatient.
'Phil, did you tell Peg what I told you?'
'Ye — s, ma'am,' says Phil, drawling out
her answer. 'Well, why don't the jade
do what I told her? Peg, come here, you
hussy! Did you tell Sue what Phil told
you?' 'Yes, ma'am.' 'Well, why don't
the lazy trollop come along? Here I am
waiting for the needle! Tell the jade to
come instantly!'

"Risum teneatis? Hold, my readers
don't know Latin; but can you help laugh-
ing, my friends? Laugh, then, at the Southern nabob, with twenty fat slaves in his

kitchen, — laugh well at him, for there is
cause enough ; then come *home* and laugh.

" You want a good school, perhaps, and
so do your neighbors. But whose business
is it to find a teacher, a house, etc. ? ' John,
I wish you would speak to William to ask
Joseph to desire our friend Daniel to set
about getting a good school. We want one
very much ; it is a shame to us to be so
negligent.' This is the last we hear of the
good school. *What is everybody's business
is nobody's.*

" You want to collect the public taxes
into the treasury of the State. The towns
choose constables or collectors of taxes. No
security is taken for a faithful discharge of
the trust, but a law is passed, which says,
like the mistress to her wenches, Treasurer,
do you tell the constable to collect and pay
over the taxes. The collector, like the nabob's slave, has no motive for diligence ; he
gets not half enough for collecting to pay
for his horse-flesh. He lounges about a year
or two, squanders away the money, and
where is his bondsman? The town! Right,
the town is his bondsman. The law says,
Treasurer, do you issue your execution

against the sheriff, and command him to
levy upon the constable, who is not worth
a farthing ; get a return of *non est inventus ;*
then levy upon his bondsman, the town ;
take the estate of everybody, post it for sale,
get it receipted and not delivered ; sue the
receipts-man, get the money, make the town
pay it twice, — 27,000l. in arrears ! It is a
shame ! Oh, such a bustle with Mr. Everybody, and all to pick up a needle ! The
State is like the nabob's family. ' Phil, tell
Peg to tell Sue to pick up the needle.'

"Now in fact it is a very easy thing to
pick up a needle, but if one cannot stoop
to pick it up another ought to be paid for
it. One servant who is paid for his work
will pick up more needles than twenty fat,
lounging slaves that think it a drudgery
and get nothing for it.

"It would be a good thing for a State to
know that *everybody's business is nobody's.*
Every man in Connecticut is responsible for
a faithful collection of public money ; then
it is nobody's business. The Prompter
never saw a watch with two mainsprings,
much less with two hundred. One spring
is enough, and that government, the execu-

tive of which depends on many springs, will
jar, clash, stop, and be always out of order,
— 27,000l. in arrears.

"Appoint one collector, the treasurer ;
make him answerable for the collection of
the whole state revenue. Let him appoint
his deputies ; let them be few, but let them
be paid. All the difficulty will vanish ; one
spring will move the whole ; the state treasury, like the federal, will be supplied ; no arrears then, no levying executions on towns."

This happens to have its application to
public affairs ; most of the twenty-eight
papers have their special point in personal
character. The writing is not elegant; it is
sometimes ungrammatical ; but it is intelligible, and with its bluntness could hardly
fail to make itself felt. It is when one compares it with similar work of Franklin's, as
" The Whistle," for example, that one is reminded of its inartistic form. But Webster
was always busy over subjects directly connected with the well-being of the people.
His philological work had its origin in this
motive, and in his miscellaneous writings
he displayed his practical philosophy and

philanthropy. He wrote frequently upon banks and banking; his "Epidemic and Pestilential Diseases" is pronounced by an authority to have great historical value; he was one of the founders of the Connecticut Academy of Arts and Sciences; and in the numerous list of his writings one comes upon such oddly assorted subjects as an account of a tornado in Wethersfield, a cure for cancer, upon white-washing, the mental arithmetic of a negro, on winds, upon female education, on the decomposition of white-lead paint, a dissertation on the supposed change in the temperature of winter, upon names of streets in New York, on yellow fever, on the age of literary men, and one article with the suggestive title "Number of Deaths in the Episcopal Church in New York in each Month for Ten Years." He had a passion for statistics which took an odd turn. In his diary one constantly finds an enumeration of the houses in the town which he happens to be visiting. "During his brief residence in New York," says one biographical sketch, "Mr. Webster numbered the houses in the city, and found that they were thirty-five

11

hundred." He would count up one side of a street and down the other, and place the results in his note-book. I think he published in some paper the record of this individual census as applied to a number of houses and villages. There must have been in his constitution an inordinate love of detail, intensified, perhaps, by much contemplation of those battalions of words which make his spelling-book pages look like spiritual armies marching against ignorance.

We have already observed Webster's interest in political discussion, and have tried to disclose something of his temper when viewing questions of public policy. " The Prompter" was written with reference to the conduct of life in individuals, but, as in the paper copied above, there is constant regard to the American character, and to the manner in which one should conduct himself in the new conditions of American life. The general subject of Americanism was one upon which he was constantly writing. We shall see later the length to which he carried his views in relation to the American language; here we may note some of the directions which his thought took when

dealing with what may be called the greater
morals of national life. In his " Remarks on
the Manners, Government, and Debt of the
United States," an odd combination of subjects, apparently, but very closely connected
in Webster's mind, he undertakes to discover the cause of some of the political evils
of the day, and is led by his subject into
regions lying outside of politics.

" A fundamental mistake of the Americans has been that they considered the revolution as completed, when it was but just
begun. Having raised the pillars of the
building, they ceased to exert themselves,
and seemed to forget that the whole super-
structure was then to be erected. This
country is independent in government, but
totally dependent in manners, which are the
basis of government. Men seem not to attend to the difference between Europe and
America in point of age and improvement,
and are disposed to rush with heedless emu-
lation into an imitation of manners for which
we are not prepared. . . .

" The present ambition of Americans is
to introduce as fast as possible the fashionable amusements of the European courts.

Considering the former dependence of America on England, her descent, her connection and present intercourse, this ambition cannot surprise us. But it must check this ambition to reflect on the consequences. It will not be denied that there are vices predominant in the most polite cities in Europe which are not only unknown, but are seldom mentioned, in America, and vices that are infamous beyond conception. I presume it will not be denied that there must be an amazing depravation of mind in a nation where a farce is a publication of more consequence than Milton's poem, and where an opera dancer, or an Italian singer, receives a salary equal to that of an ambassador. The facts being known and acknowledged, I presume the consequence will not be denied. Not that the charge is good against every individual; even in the worst times there will be found many exceptions to the general character of a nation. . . .

"In some Asiatic countries people never change their mode of dress. This uniformity, which continues for ages, proceeds from the same principles as the monthly changes in England and France; both proceed from necessity and policy. Both arise from good causes which operate in the several governments; that is, the manners of each government are subservient to its particular interest. The reverse is true of this country. Our manners are wholly subservient to the interest of foreign nations. Where do we find, in dress or equipage, the least reference to the circumstances of this country? Is it not the sole ambition of the Americans to be just like other nations, without the means of supporting the resemblance? We ought not to harbor any spleen or prejudice against foreign kingdoms. This would be illiberal. They are wise, they are respectable. We should despise the man that piques himself on his own country, and treats all others with indiscriminate contempt. I wish to see much less jealousy and ill-nature subsisting between the Americans and English. But in avoiding party spirit and resentment on the one hand, we should be very careful of servility on the other. There is a manly pride in true independence which is equally remote from insolence and meanness, — a pride that is characteristic of great minds. Have Americans discovered this pride since the declaration of peace? We boast of independence, and with propriety. But will not the same men who glory in this great event, even in the midst of a gasconade, turn to a foreigner, and ask him, 'What is the latest fashion in Europe?' He has worn an elegant suit of clothes for six weeks; he might wear it a few weeks longer, but it has not so many buttons as the last suit of my Lord ——. He throws it aside, and gets one that has. The suit costs him a sum of money; but it keeps him in the fashion, and feeds the poor of Great Britain or France. It is a singular phenomenon, and to posterity it will appear incredible, that a nation of heroes, who have conquered armies and raised an empire, should not have the spirit to say, *We will wear our clothes as we please.*

"Let it not be thought that this is a trifling subject, a matter of no consequence. Mankind are governed by opinion; and while we flatter ourselves that we enjoy independence because no foreign power can impose laws upon us, we are groaning beneath the tyranny of opinion, — a tyranny more severe than the laws of monarchs; a

dominion, voluntary, indeed, but, for that
reason, more effectual ; an authority of manners, which commands our services, and
sweeps away the fruits of our labor.

" I repeat the sentiment with which I began, — the Revolution of America is yet
incomplete. We are now in a situation to
answer all the purposes of the European nations, — independent in government, and
dependent in manners. They give us their
fashions ; they direct our taste to make a
market for their commodities ; they engross
the profits of our industry, without the hazard of defending us, or the expense of supporting our civil government. A situation
more favorable to their interest or more re-
pugnant to our own they could not have
chosen for us, nor we embraced."

" Every man in New England is a theologian," says Webster in the passage quoted
at the head of this chapter, and Webster
himself was no exception to his statement.
He published in " The Panoplist," and afterward in pamphlet form, " The Peculiar
Doctrines of the Gospel Explained and Defended," an apology for Calvinism, which

drew out an answer by "An Old-fashioned Churchman." With more direct reference to his special pursuits, he published "Mistakes and Corrections in the Common Version of the Scriptures, in the Hebrew Lexicon of Gesenius, and in Richardson's Dictionary."

The most considerable venture which Webster made in this field was in his edition of the Bible. He was a Revision Committee of one, and went to work with his customary self-confidence not to retranslate the Bible, but to correct and improve its English, "with amendments of the language," the title-page declares. His reasons for undertaking the work and his principles of revision are given in the preface to his edition, which was published at New Haven in 1833 : —

. . . "In the present [King James] version, the language is, in general, correct and perspicuous ; the genuine popular English of Saxon origin ; peculiarly adapted to the subjects ; and in many passages uniting sublimity with beautiful simplicity. In my view, the general style of the version ought not to be altered. But in the lapse of two or three centuries changes have taken place, which in particular passages impair the beauty, in others obscure the sense, of the original languages. Some words have fallen into disuse; and the signification of others, in current popular use, is not the same now as it was when they were introduced into the version. The effect of these changes is that some words are not understood by common readers, who have no access to commentaries, and who will always compose a great proportion of readers; while other words, being now used in a sense different from that which they had when the translation was made, present a wrong signification or false ideas. Whenever words are understood in a sense different from that which they had when introduced, and different from that of the original languages, they do not present to the reader the Word of God. This circumstance is very important, even in things not the most essential; and in essential points mistakes may be very injurious. In my own view of this subject, a version of the Scriptures for popular use should consist of words expressing the sense which is most

common in popular usage, so that the first
ideas suggested to the reader should be the
true meaning of such words according to
the original languages. That many words
in the present version fail to do this is certain. My principal aim is to remedy this
evil. . . .

"In performing this task I have been
careful to avoid unnecessary innovations,
and to retain the general character of the
style. The principal alterations are com-
prised in three classes : —

"1. The substitution of words and phrases
now in good use for such as are wholly obsolete, or deemed below the dignity and
solemnity of the subject.

"2. The correction of errors in grammar.

"3. The insertion of euphemisms, words
and phrases which are not very offensive to
delicacy, in the place of such as cannot, with
propriety, be uttered before a promiscuous
audience."

All this has a most familiar sound to-
day, and when Webster goes on with a plea
for consideration and a doubt as to how his
necessary work will be received, we seem
to hear again the apologies and defenses

with which the press has of late been filled.
People have used the Bible so long, Webster observes, that they have acquired a
predilection for its quaintnesses. "It may
require," he continues, "some effort to sub-
due this predilection; but it may be done,
and for the sake of the rising generation it
is desirable. . . . As there are diversities
of tastes among men, it is not to be expected
that the alterations I have made in the language of the version will please all classes
of readers. Some persons will think I have
done too little; others, too much. And
probably the result would be the same,
were a revision to be executed by any other
hand, or even by the joint labors of many
hands. All I can say is that I have executed this work in the manner which, in my
judgment, appeared to be the best. . . . In
this undertaking I subject myself to the
charge of arrogance; but I am not conscious
of being actuated by any improper motive.
I am aware of the sensitiveness of the religious public on this subject, and of the difficulties which attend the performance. But
all men whom I have consulted, if they have
thought much on the subject, seem to be

agreed in the opinion that it is high time
to have a revision of the common version of
the Scriptures; although no person appears
to know how or by whom such a revision is
to be executed. In my own view, such revision is not merely a matter of expedience,
but of moral duty; and as I have been encouraged to undertake this work by respectable literary and religious characters, I have
ventured to attempt a revision upon my own
responsibility. If the work should fail to
be well received, the loss will be my own,
and I hope no injury will be done. I have
been painfully solicitous that no error should
escape me."

It is not difficult to understand Webster's
attitude. He is a school-master in this business, squaring Elizabethan English to suit
the regularity and uniformity of language
which have been the dream of all school-
masters. Rules without exceptions repre-
sent the unattainable ideal of mechanical
minds. Webster, vainly endeavoring to reduce language to an orderly system, was
also moved to secure propriety and decorum.
He seems, therefore, to have gone through
the book with his pen, transposing words

into a more formal order, removing quaintnesses, changing old forms into current ones,
putting on fig leaves, and, so far as he dared,
shaving the language to fit the measure of
the speech of his day. But he did not undertake the work as a scholar, aiming at a
more exact version, and his emendations,
where the sense would be at all affected,
were very inconsiderable. He changed, to
be sure, *take no thought* into *be not anxious,*
as the Revisers have done, and he incorporated into the text the marginal reading
to them for *by them* in the passage, *Ye have
heard that it hath been said by them of old
times.* He substituted *demons* for *devils,*
as the American Committee preferred; he
tried to put *hell* in its proper place, and in
some trivial instances he was more exact in
his use of prepositions, but one would look
in vain for any sign of Hebrew or Greek
scholarship beyond the most rudimentary.

Nor in respect of English did he seem to
have any conception of style or color; he
patched clauses with words of his time,
when he desired to remove an obsolete expression, without any sense, apparently, of
incongruousness, and he removed words

which were still perfectly clear in meaning, only because they would not in his day so be used. He was very much disturbed by what he regarded as inelegance, and picturesque phrases or words were likely to give way to more commonplace ones. He did not like *gather together* and substituted the more rotund *assemble, collect,* or *convene; three score* he wrote *sixty;* he hustled out the strong phrase *gave up the ghost,* and put in its place the " elegant " *expire; peradventure* yielded to *perhaps* or *it may be; laugh to scorn* he wrote *deride.* A good example of his indifference to racy English is in his substituting *in health* for *safe and sound* in the clause, *because he hath received him safe and sound.* " This is another instance," he writes in his Introduction, " in which the translators have followed popular use instead of the original Greek, which signifies simply *well* or *in health.*"

Some of his alterations were in the direction of greater intelligibility. He used *button* instead of *tache, capital* for *chapiter,* and made Hebrew proper names in the New Testament conform to the usage of the Old. " This will prevent illiterate persons, who compose a large part of the readers of the Scriptures, from mistaking the characters. Every obstacle to a right understanding of the Scriptures, however small, should be removed, when it can be done in consistency with truth." Like the American Committee he preferred *Holy Spirit* to *Holy Ghost*, and was willing to drop the title *Saint* from the names of the evangelists, and having all the authority necessary he made these changes. In other instances there appears an interesting agreement between this independent American reviser of 1833 and the American Committee of the present year; number VII. of the classes of passages recorded at the close of the Revised version, as preferred by the American Committee, reads: "Substitute modern forms of speech for the following archaisms, namely, *who* or *that* for *which* when used of persons ; *are* for *be* in the present indicative ; *know, knew*, for *wot, wist; drag* or *drag away* for *hale*," and Webster's corrections upon the same plan are uniform. It is unquestionably due to Webster that the American Committee had this preference, not to the Webster who revised the Bible, for it is scarcely likely that his revision was used for reference, but to the Webster who early proposed such changes in the use of language and never ceased to urge them upon every occasion. So, too, both agree in dropping *thy way* from the phrase *go thy way ;* in saying *urgent* for *instant.* The variations, however, of the American Committee from the English have reference largely to readings.

The great bulk of Webster's emendations were of the most trivial and innocent character. *Whosoever* and *whatsoever* he always cut down by the omission of the second syllable ; *unto* and *until* he changed to *to* and *till ; wherein* and its fellows he usually rendered by *in which, on which, in that* or *this ; ate* he preferred to *did eat ;* and *yes* to *yea.* It was in general a picayune revision, sufficient to annoy those who had an ear for the old version, and really offering only such positive helps in interpretation as were generally in the possession of fairly educated men. That he should have done the work at all and have done it so faintly is what surprises the reader. As a commercial undertaking it was no mean matter, and it was followed by the publication of an edition of the New Testament alone. What a strange miscalculation of forces it appears to have been! It implied that readers generally were as much martinets in language as the editor, and it did not take into account the immense inertia to be overcome, when a single man should undertake to set aside the accumulated reverence of two centuries. The revision of the Bible by Webster was in singular confirmation of traits of character which have already been noted. He had unlimited confidence in himself, an almost childish ignorance of obstacles, a persistence which was unembarrassed by the indifference of others, and, from his long continued occupation, a habit of magnifying the trivial. He had not, in such a work as this, the qualifications of a scholar; he had simply the training of a school-master; he was ignorant of what he was undertaking, and his independent revision of the Bible failed to win attention, not because it was audacious, but because it was not bold enough; it offered no real contribution to Biblical criticism.

He secured for it, indeed, a certain en-

dorsement. A testimonial, signed by the
president and the most distinguished members of the faculty of Yale College, recites
cautiously : "Dr. Webster's edition of the
Bible, in which the language of the translation is purified from obsolete, ungrammatical, and exceptional words and phrases, is
approved and used by many clergymen and
other gentlemen very competent to judge
of its merits," an ingenious form of words
which, I hope, satisfied Dr. Webster. Others, chiefly his neighbors in New Haven,
signed more elaborate documents, intended,
apparently, to meet objections and prejudices against a changed Bible. Webster himself declared to the editors of a religious
paper, whom he suspected to be unfriendly
to his design, "I consider this emendation
of the common version as the most important enterprise of my life, and as important
as any benevolent design now on foot; and
I feel much hurt that my friends should dis-
countenance the design." This was written
a few months after the publication of the
work. Eight years later, when he was in the
eighty-fourth year of his age, he still clung
to the hope that his work might be accepted

and put to general use ; he had already in his will bequeathed to each of his grandchildren a copy of the book " handsomely bound," the only one of his publications thus marked by his favor, and the letter which at this time, a year before his death, he addressed to the Members of the Eastern Association, in New Haven County, shows no abatement in his faith.

"NEW HAVEN, *May* 19, 1842.

"GENTLEMEN : My edition of the Bible, with emendations of the language of the common version, has been before the public about eight years. I have heard no objection to the manner in which the work has been executed, and, as far as my information extends, the work is generally approved by those who have examined it, among whom are many clergymen, whose special duty it is to guard the sacred text from corruption. The body of the language in the common version was introduced by Tyndale more than three hundred and twenty years ago. In the great length of time that has since elapsed, the language has suffered many material changes, some of which affect the sense of passages, rendering it obscure or unintelligible to the unlettered part of readers. Some passages are perverted by the use of wrong words, the grammatical errors are numerous, and many passages are expressed in language which decency forbids to be repeated in families and the pulpit. For these reasons it appears to me that a due regard to the interest of religion requires a revision of the common version. Indeed, all men seem to agree that amendments are wanted, but who shall undertake the work? So numerous are the denominations of Christians that no one would undertake it without the concurrence of others, unless for sectarian purposes, and there is no probability that a concurrence of all could be obtained. For these reasons it seems to be obvious, that if any improvement is to be made in the version, the work must be done by an individual. It is my desire that the association shall take into consideration the propriety of rendering me their active aid in prompting the use of the amended copy of the Bible in families and schools. I am, gentlemen, with much respect, your obedient servant,

" N. WEBSTER."

His judgment has been partially confirmed, partially set aside. One denomination did undertake a revision and failed; but contrary to Webster's belief it has been found possible to obtain the concurrence of different bodies of men for a revision which comes with weight, and receives an attention not to be secured by testimonials of county associations. There was a wide difference between Webster's conception of a revision and that entertained by the distinguished scholars who carried forward the recent one. I wonder if one of those scholars who signed the non-committal endorsement of Webster's Bible may not, in the midst of his recent labors, have contrasted in his mind the learned company to which he belonged with the school-master who offered a Bible "purified from the numerous errors."

CHAPTER VI.

PREPARATION FOR THE DICTIONARY.

IT is not an uncommon experience by which a young man strikes at once the note of his career, then appears to wander or experiment, and returns more surely to his original expression, following that steadily to the end. It was thus with Webster. His "Grammatical Institute," inclosing the perennial speller, was his first declaration; then he made ventures in different directions, but returned to studies in language, and finally embodied the results of his lifetime in his great Dictionary. In reading biography, we wish to get at the ruling passion of the man; how often the man himself seems bewildered in his search for it, groping in this direction and in that, uncertain, to use Dr. Bushnell's vigorous phrase, if he has yet grasped the handle of his being. It cannot be said that Webster ever laid aside his special studies and

resumed them after long intervals. His
earliest and most characteristic work, " A
Grammatical Institute," was always by him,
and the Speller, which emerged from it, became of so much pecuniary importance that
it could not fail to determine in many ways
his occupation. The " Minerva" from the
first had constant advertisements both of
" A Grammatical Institute " and of the early
volume of " Dissertations"; there were frequent announcements of new editions of
the Spelling-Book, and of the rate at which
it could be had in quantities. Country
merchants began to lay in supplies of Webster's Spelling-Book, when they came to the
nearest trading town, as confidently as they
bought West India goods or English tools.
Webster gave lectures, as he traveled north
and south, upon the English language. His
reputation was forming upon this line, and
it is not unlikely that his partial failure
in political and journalistic work was due
to his identification with the occupation of
a school-master. A more complete account
would be that he did not do these things
thoroughly well, because his strongest at-
traction was in another direction. He seems,

through the twenty years or more which followed the first publication of his Spelling-Book, to have his hand close by the throttle-lever without knowing it. The practical demands of self-support no doubt controlled his inclinations, and forced him into one situation after another where his choice would not send him, and he spent these years in a struggle for maintenance. Then he was an impulsive, a generous, and an ambitious man. He loved society; he liked the stir of men and the bustle of management. As we have already seen, he was ready to venture all he had upon the stakes which his ardor set up. He took risks in publishing, which could be justified only by his own enthusiasm, and entertained himself with speculations in literature which were agreeable to contemplate, but often disastrous to realize. There is a half-despairing letter to Josiah Quincy [1] which discloses the hard lines of his practical life. Trumbull had jested at Webster's slight capital for housekeeping, and Webster himself reached points in his career where even Institutes and Dissertations seemed to fail him. The letter

[1] In the possession of Rev. R. C. Waterston.

is dated at New Haven, February 12, 1811. He writes with some irritation, " My name has been so much bandied about that I am quite willing it should be seen and heard no more at present," and then passes to the more important matters in his mind : " I am engaged in a work which gives me great pleasure, and the tracing of language through more than twenty different dialects has opened a new and before unexplored field. I have within two years past made discoveries which, if ever published, must interest the literati of all Europe, and render it necessary to revise all the lexicons — Hebrew, Greek, and Latin — now used as classical books. But what can I do? My own resources are almost exhausted, and in a few days I shall sell my house to get bread for my children. All the assurances of aid which I had received in Boston, New York, etc., have failed, and I am soon to retire to a humble cottage in the country. To add to my perplexity, the political measures pursuing render it almost impossible to sell property, or to obtain money upon the best security. A few thousand dollars, for which I can give security, would place me in a con-

dition in the country to live with comfort
and pursue my studies; but even this cannot be obtained till the measures of Congress assume a more auspicious aspect.
Adieu, dear sir. The little Band will no
doubt do their duty, but what can be done
against the army of slaves? Alexander
Wolcott!! We must drink the cup of disgrace to the dregs! Yours, in low spirits,
"N. WEBSTER, JUN."

If the letter was an indirect appeal to
Mr. Quincy to advance a few thousand dollars on good security, it does not seem to
have effected its purpose, and a man with
money to lend would not have his confidence in the borrower's capacity to repay it
increased by knowing that the time of the
loan was to be occupied in making astonishing discoveries in the roots of language. It
has often been stated that Dr. Webster supported himself and large family, during the
twenty or thirty years he was employed in
the preparation of his great Dictionary,
mainly by a copyright of one cent or less
on his Spelling-Book, and it is quite certain
that the several other enterprises in which

he engaged never supported him while they were going on, and often resulted in losses. But what a picture the letter presents of an impecunious scholar, bewitched by his pursuit, and sure that it was to end in some vast result! He writes like an inventor who needs but little to enable him to perfect a machine which is to revolutionize labor.

It was only a few years after the first publication of the Spelling-Book, and while Webster was still unmarried and trying his hand at various occupations, that he published " A Collection of Essays and Fugitiv Writings on Moral, Historical, Political, and Literary Subjects." The short-tailed word on the title-page is an oddity intended probably to attract the reader's attention and lead him to look within. The contents embrace thirty essays, originally written or published between the years 1787 and 1790, but before the reader comes upon the table of contents he is likely to stop at the Preface with its antics of spelling. We are tolerably used by this time to reformed spelling, but Webster was a pioneer, and his contemporaries must have looked with some amazement at what they could only think of as deformed spelling. Here they could be told soberly : —

" During the course of ten or twelv yeers I hav been laboring to correct popular errors, and to assist my yung brethren in the road to truth and virtue; my publications for theez purposes hav been numerous; much time haz been spent, which I do not regret, and much censure incurred, which my hart tells me I do not dezerv. The influence of a yung writer cannot be so powerful or extensiv az that of an established karacter; but I hav ever thot a man's usefulness depends more on exertion than on talents. I am attached to America by berth, education, and habit; but abuv all, by a philosophical view of her situation, and the superior advantages she enjoys, for augmenting the sum of social happiness. . . .

" The reeder will obzerv that the orthography of the volum iz not uniform. The reezon iz, that many of the essays hav been published before, in the common orthography, and it would hav been a laborious task to copy the whole, for the sake of changing the spelling.

"In the essays ritten within the last yeer, a considerable change of spelling iz introduced by way of experiment. This liberty waz taken by the writers before the age of Queen Elizabeth, and to this we are indeted for the preference of modern spelling over that of Gower and Chaucer. The man who admits that the change of *housbonde, mynde, ygone, moneth* into husband, mind, gone, month, iz an improovment, must acknowledge also the riting of helth, breth, rong, tung, munth, to be an improovment. There iz no alternativ. Every possible reezon that could ever be offered for altering the spelling of wurds, stil exists in full force; and if a gradual reform should not be made in our language, it will proov that we are less under the influence of reezon than our ancestors."

This passage from the Preface, as well as those papers in the volume which follow the same style of orthography or rather cacography, will illustrate well enough the unprincipled character of the reform as it lay in Webster's mind. He acted upon the merest empiricism apparently, without any well-considered plan, making the spelling occasionally conform to the sound, but allowing even the same sounds to have different representation in different words. Indeed, in the extract given above, he appears to be rather a timid reformer, attacking such defenseless little words as *is*, and respectfully passing by *would* and *offered*. The general appearance of those essays in the volume which are printed after Webster's own heart leads one happening upon them nowadays into some disappointment, since they are by no means to be ranked with the humorous writings of later misspellers, who have contrived to get some fun out of venerable words by pulling off their wigs and false teeth and turning them loose in the streets.

It is very likely that Webster's first impulse to reform our spelling was given by Dr. Franklin's writings on the subject. As is well known, that philosopher went so far as to devise new characters for compound letters such as *th*, *sh*, *ng*, anticipating many of the later experiment in phonic writing. Webster entered with zeal into the notion, and held a correspondence with Franklin, in which the young man showed himself so

ardent a disciple of the old as to win for
himself a certain place as the doctor's re-
siduary legatee in ideas. "This indefatigable gentleman," says Webster of Franklin, "amidst all his other employments,
public and private, has compiled a Dictionary on his scheme of a reform, and procured types to be cast for printing it. He
thinks himself too old to pursue the plan;
but has honored me with the offer of the
manuscript and types, and expressed a
strong desire that I should undertake the
task. Whether this project, so deeply interesting to this country, will ever be effected, or whether it will be defeated by indolence and prejudice, remains for my countrymen to determine." The last clause,
with all its obscurity, may be taken as a
threat rather than as a self-reproach. The
entire correspondence between Webster and
Franklin is interesting as setting forth a certain excess of experimenting ardor in Franklin and an unlooked-for degree of conser-
vatism in Webster. Franklin was the older
man, but he was the more daring. One
should credit him, however, with a certain
amount of humor in his whims. He played

with the English language, somewhat as he amused himself with conferring legacies at compound interest, to take effect in two hundred years, and giving away gravely millions of money by the immediate planting of a few hundreds.

If the first impulse came from Franklin, the controlling reason must be looked for in Webster's patriotism. It was no trifling desire to put into practice an engaging theory, but a conviction of public gain which moved Webster to proclaim his reform. He has left abundant testimony to this effect. After giving a brief historical sketch of the changes to which the English language had been subjected, in the Appendix to his " Dissertations," he proceeds : —

" The question now occurs : ought the Americans to retain these faults which produce innumerable inconveniences in the acquisition and use of the language, or ought they at once to reform these abuses, and introduce order and regularity into the orthography of the AMERICAN TONGUE ? " He throws all the emphasis possible upon these words by the use of large type, and

then sketches the nature of the proposed
reform, returning in the conclusion to his
favorite position of the influence upon national speech and manners.

The whole statement is so interesting,
especially when taken into comparison with
the recent declarations of war by eminent
American philologists, that I transfer it to
these pages.

" Several attempts were formerly made in
England to rectify the orthography of the
language.[1] But I apprehend their schemes
failed of success rather on account of their
intrinsic difficulties than on account of any
necessary impracticability of a reform. It
was proposed, in most of these schemes, not
merely to throw out superfluous and silent
letters, but to introduce a number of new
characters. Any attempt on such a plan
must undoubtedly prove unsuccessful. It is
not to be expected that an orthography,

[1] " The first by Sir Thomas Smith, secretary of state
to Queen Elizabeth; another by Dr. Gill, a celebrated
master of St. Paul's School in London; another by Mr.
Charles Butler, who went so far as to print his book in
his proposed orthography; several in the time of Charles
the first; and in the present age, Mr. Elphinstone has
published a treatise in a very ridiculous orthography."

13

perfectly regular and simple, such as would
be formed by a ' Synod of Grammarians on
principles of science,' will ever be substituted for that confused mode of spelling
which is now established. But it is appre-
hended that great improvements may be
made, and an orthography almost regular,
or such as shall obviate most of the present
difficulties which occur in learning our language, may be introduced and established
with little trouble and opposition. The
principal alterations necessary to render our
orthography regular and easy are these :

" 1. The omission of all superfluous or
silent letters ; as *a* in *bread*. Thus *bread,
head, give, breast, built, meant, realm,
friend*, would be spelt *bred, hed, giv, brest,
bilt, ment, relm, frend*. Would this alteration produce any inconvenience, any embarrassment or expense ? By no means. On
the other hand, it would lessen the trouble
of writing, and, much more, of learning the
language ; it would reduce the true pronunciation to a certainty ; and while it
would assist foreigners and our own children in acquiring the language, it would
render the pronunciation uniform in dif-

ferent parts of the country, and almost prevent the possibility of changes.

"2. A substitution of a character that has a certain definite sound for one that is more vague and indeterminate. Thus by putting *ee* instead of *ea* or *ie*, the words *mean, near, speak, grieve, zeal*, would become *meen, neer, speek, greev, zeel*. This alteration could not occasion a moment's trouble; at the same time it would prevent a doubt respecting the pronunciation; whereas the *ea* and *ie*, having different sounds, may give a learner much difficulty. Thus *greef* should be substituted for *grief*; *kee* for *key*; *beleev* for *believe*; *laf* for *laugh*; *dawter* for *daughter*; *plow* for *plough*; *tuf* for *tough*; *proov* for *prove*; *blud* for *blood*; and *draft* for *draught*. In this manner *ch* in Greek derivatives should be changed into *k*; for the English *ch* has a soft sound as in *cherish*; but *k* always a hard sound. Therefore *character, chorus, colic, architecture*, should be written *karacter, korus, kolic, arkitecture*, and were they thus written no person could mistake their true pronunciation. Thus *ch* in French derivatives should be changed into *sh*; *machine, chaise, chev-*

alier, should be written *masheen*, *shaze*, *shevaleer*, and *pique*, *tour*, *oblique*, should be written *peek*, *toor*, *obleek*.

"3. A trifling alteration in a character, or the addition of a point, would distinguish different sounds without the substitution of a new character. Thus a very small stroke across *th* would distinguish its two sounds. A point over a vowel in this manner, *à* or *ò* or *ī*, might answer all the purposes of different letters. And for the diphthong *ow* let the two letters be united by a small stroke, or both engraven on the same piece of metal, with the left hand line of the *w* united to the *o*. These, with a few other inconsiderable alterations, would answer every purpose, and render the orthography sufficiently correct and regular.

"The advantages to be derived from these alterations are numerous, great, and permanent.

"1. The simplicity of the orthography would facilitate the learning of the language. It is now the work of years for children to learn to spell; and after all, the business is rarely accomplished. A few men, who are bred to some business that requires constant exercise in writing, finally learn to spell most words without hesitation ; but most people remain all their lives imperfect masters of spelling, and liable to make mistakes whenever they take up a pen to write a short note. Nay, many people, even of education and fashion, never attempt to write a letter without frequently consulting a dictionary. But with the proposed orthography, a child would learn to spell, without trouble, in a very short time, and the orthography being very regular, he would ever after find it difficult to make a mistake. It would, in that case, be as difficult to spell *wrong* as it is now to spell *right*. Besides this advantage, foreigners would be able to acquire the pronunciation of English, which is now so difficult and embarrassing that they are either wholly discouraged on the first attempt, or obliged, after many years' labor, to rest contented with an imperfect knowledge of the subject.

" 2. A correct orthography would render the pronunciation of the language as uniform as the spelling in books. A general uniformity thro the United States would be the event of such a reformation as I am here recommending. All persons, of every rank, would speak with some degree of precision and uniformity. Such a uniformity in these States is very desirable; it would remove prejudice, and conciliate mutual affection and respect.

" 3. Such a reform would diminish the number of letters about one sixteenth or eighteenth. This would save a page in eighteen; and a saving of an eighteenth in the expense of books is an advantage that should not be overlooked.

" 4. But a capital advantage of this reform in these States would be, that it would make a difference between the English orthography and the American. This will startle those who have not attended to the subject; but I am confident that such an event is an object of vast political consequence. For,

" The alteration, however small, would encourage the publication of books in our own country. It would render it, in some measure, necessary that all books should be printed in America. The English would never copy our orthography for their own use; and consequently the same impressions of books would not answer for both countries. The inhabitants of the present generation would read the English impressions; but posterity, being taught a different spelling, would prefer the American orthography.

"Besides this, a *national language* is a band of *national union.* Every engine should be employed to render the people of this country *national;* to call their attachments home to their own country; and to inspire them with the pride of national character. However they may boast of independence, and the freedom of their government, yet their *opinions* are not sufficiently independent; an astonishing respect for the arts and literature of their parent country, and a blind imitation of its manners, are still prevalent among the Americans. Thus an habitual respect for another country, deserved indeed and once laudable, turns their attention from their own interests, and prevents their respecting themselves."

He supposes various objections to this reform: that it would oblige people to relearn

the language; that it would render present
books useless; that it would injure the language by obscuring etymology; that the
distinction between words of different mean-
ings and similar sound would be destroyed;
that it was idle to conform the orthography
of words to the pronunciation, because the
latter was continually changing. All these
objections he considers and meets with arguments more familiar to us than they were to
men of his day, and then concludes: —

"Sensible I am how much easier it is
to *propose* improvements than to *introduce*
them. Everything new starts the idea of
difficulty, and yet it is often mere novelty
that excites the appearance; for on a slight
examination of the proposal the difficulty
vanishes. When we firmly believe a scheme
to be practicable, the work is half accomplished. We are more frequently deterred
by fear from making an attack, than re-
pulsed in the encounter.

"Habit also is opposed to changes, for it
renders even our errors dear to us. Having surmounted all difficulties in childhood,
we forget the labor, the fatigue, and the
perplexity we suffered in the attempt, and

imagine the progress of our studies to have
been smooth and easy. What seems in-
trinsically right is so merely thro habit.
Indolence is another obstacle to improvements. The most arduous task a reformer
has to execute is to make people *think;* to
rouse them from that lethargy, which, like
the mantle of sleep, covers them in repose
and contentment.

"But America is in a situation the most
favorable for great reformations; and the
present time is, in a singular degree, auspicious. The minds of men in this country
have been awakened. New scenes have
been, for many years, presenting new occasions for exertion; unexpected distresses
have called forth the powers of invention;
and the application of new expedients has
demanded every possible exercise of wisdom and talents. Attention is roused, the
mind expanded, and the intellectual faculties invigorated. Here men are prepared
to receive improvements, which would be
rejected by nations whose habits have not
been shaken by similar events.

"*Now* is the time, and *this* the country,
in which we may expect success in attempt-

ing changes favorable to language, science, and government. Delay in the plan here proposed may be fatal; under a tranquil general government the minds of men may again sink into indolence ; a national acquiescence in error will follow, and posterity be doomed to struggle with difficulties which time and accident will perpetually multiply.

" Let us, then, seize the present moment and establish a *national language* as well as a national government. Let us remember that there is a certain respect due to the opinions of other nations. As an independent people, our reputation abroad demands that, in all things, we should be federal, be *national ;* for, if we do not respect ourselves, we may be assured that other nations will not respect us. In short, let it be impressed upon the mind of every American, that to neglect the means of commanding respect abroad is treason against the character and dignity of a brave, independent people."

In the matter of pronunciation, Webster asserted similar principles in his earliest essays. He denounces the custom of referring to English standards for the determination of sounds. In the " Remarks on the Manners, Government, and Debt of the United States," which I quoted in the last chapter, he finds fault with his countrymen for their dependence upon England.

" This same veneration for eminent foreigners and the bewitching charms of fashion have led the Americans to adopt the modern corruptions of our language. Very seldom have men examined the structure of the language to find reasons for their practice. The pronunciation and use of words have been subject to the same arbitrary or accidental changes as the shape of their garments. My lord wears a hat of a certain size and shape ; he pronounces a word in a certain manner ; and both must be right, for he is a fashionable man. In Europe this is right in dress ; and men who have not an opportunity of learning the just rules of our language are in some degree excusable for imitating those whom they consider as superiors. But in men of science this imitation can hardly be excused. Our language was spoken in purity about eighty years ago, since which time great numbers of faults have crept into practice about the theatre and court of London. An affected, erroneous pronunciation has in many instances taken place of the true, and new words or modes of speech have succeeded the ancient correct English phrases. Thus we have, in the modern English pronunciation, their natshures, conjunctshures, constitshutions, and tshumultshuous legislatshures, and a long catalogue of fashionable improprieties. These are a direct violation of the rules of analogy and harmony; they offend the ear and embarrass the language. Time was when these errors were unknown; they were little known in America before the Revolution. I presume we may safely say that our language has suffered more injurious changes in America, since the British army landed on our shores, than it had suffered before in the period of three centuries. The bucks and bloods tell us that there is no proper standard in language; that it is all arbitrary. The assertion, however, seems but to show their ignorance. There are, in the language itself, decisive reasons for preferring one pronunciation to another; and men of science should be acquainted with these reasons. But if there were none, and everything rested on practice, we should never change a general practice without substantial reasons. No change should be introduced which is not an obvious improvement."

Elsewhere, in a similar spirit, he writes: "Nothing but the establishment of schools and some uniformity in the use of books can annihilate differences in speaking, and preserve the purity of the American tongue. A sameness of pronunciation is of considerable consequence in a political view, for provincial accents are disagreeable to strangers, and sometimes have an unhappy effect upon the social affections. . . . As an independent nation our honor requires us to have a system of our own, in language as well as government. Great Britain, whose children we are, and whose language we speak, should no longer be our standard; for the taste of her writers is already corrupted, and her language on the decline. But if it were not so, she is at too great a distance to be our model, and to instruct us in the principles of our own tongue. . . . Rapid changes of language proceed from violent causes, but these causes cannot be supposed to exist in North America. It is contrary to all rational calculation that the United States will ever be conquered by any one nation speaking a different language from that of the country. Removed from the danger of corruption by conquest, our language can change only with the slow operation of the causes before mentioned, and the progress of arts and sciences, unless the folly of imitating our parent country should continue to govern us and lead us into endless innovation. This folly, however, will lose its influence gradually, as our particular habits of respect for that country shall wear away, and our *amor patriæ* acquire strength, and inspire us with a suitable respect for our own national character. We have, therefore, the fairest opportunity of establishing a national language, and of giving it uniformity and perspicuity in North America, that ever presented itself to mankind."

His standard of pronunciation is thus defined: "The rules of the language itself, and the general practice of the nation, constitute propriety in speaking. If we examine the structure of any language we shall find a certain principle of analogy running through the whole. We shall find in English that similar combinations of letters have usually the same pronunciation, and that words having the same terminating syllable generally have the accent at the same distance from that termination. These principles of analogy were not the result of design; they must have been the effect of accident, or that tendency which all men feel toward uniformity. But the principles, when established, are productive of great convenience, and become an authority superior to the arbitrary decisions of any man or class of men. There is one exception only to this remark: When a deviation from analogy has become the universal practice of a nation, it then takes place of all rules, and becomes the standard of propriety. The two points, therefore, which I conceive to be the basis of a standard in speaking are these: universal, undisputed practice, and the principle of analogy. Universal practice is generally, perhaps always, a rule of propriety; and in disputed points, where people differ in opinion and practice, analogy should always decide the controversy.

" There are authorities to which all men will submit; they are superior to the opin-

ions and caprices of the great, and to the
negligence and ignorance of the multitude.
The authority of individuals is always liable
to be called in question ; but the unanimous
consent of a nation, and a fixed principle interwoven with the very construction of a
language, coeval and coextensive with it,
are like the common laws of a land, or the
immutable rules of morality, the propriety
of which every man, however refractory, is
forced to acknowledge, and to which most
men will readily submit."

Here is the doctrine of majorities, and
it will be seen that Webster's conception
of usage is not the usage of the most cultivated, but the general usage of a people.
It was the democratic principle carried to
its utmost length, and yet the notion of an
inhering law was quite as strongly held.
Our interest in this portion of his work is
in the examples which he gives of the usage
of his day. He points out a number of instances in which the different sections of
the Union were at variance, and some of
these characteristics have certainly disappeared.   Webster's memoranda may be
taken with some confidence, for he was a

minute observer, and his opportunities of comparison were excellent.

In the Eastern States he finds a good many people saying *motive;* in the Middle States some who say *prejudice. E* before *r* is often pronounced like *a*, as *marcy* for *mercy*, an error which he refers rather illogically to the practice of calling the letter *r ar*, so that in his Spelling-Book he writes its sound *er;* "in a few instances," he says, "this pronunciation is become general among polite speakers, as *clerk, sergeant,* etc." In calling attention to the New England custom of preferring the sound of *i* short or *e* before the diphthong *ow*, as in *kiow* for *cow*, Webster gravely refers the disagreeable peculiarity "to the nature of their government and a distribution of their property." Let the reader reflect a moment before he reads Webster's philosophical explanation, and see if his own cogitations lead him in the right direction. "It is an undoubted fact that the drawling nasal manner of speaking in New England arises almost solely from these causes. People of large fortunes, who pride themselves on family distinctions, possess a certain boldness, dig-

14

nity, and independence in their manners, which give a corresponding air to their mode of speaking. Those who are accustomed to command slaves form a habit of expressing themselves with the tone of authority and decision. In New England, where there are few slaves and servants, and less family distinctions than in any other part of America, the people are accustomed to address each other with that diffidence, or attention to the opinion of others, which marks a state of equality. Instead of commanding, they advise; instead of saying, with an air of decision, *you must;* they ask, with an air of doubtfulness, *is it not best?* or give their opinions with an indecisive tone; *You had better, I believe.* Not possessing that pride and consciousness of superiority which attend birth and fortune, their intercourse with each other is all conducted on the idea of equality, which gives a singular tone to their language and complexion to their manners. . . . Such are the causes of the local peculiarities in pronunciation which prevail among the country people in New England, and which, to foreigners, are the objects of ridicule. The great error in their manner of speaking proceeds immediately from not opening the mouth sufficiently. Hence words are drawled out in a careless lazy manner, or the sound finds a passage thro the nose."

This may have the merit of ingenuity, but in connection with it Webster makes a sounder observation when he compares New England perpetuating old English idioms because of her isolation, to an internal village contrasted with a city. " New England has been in the situation of an island ; during one hundred and sixty years, the people, except in a few commercial towns, have not been exposed to any of the causes which effect great changes in language and manners."

To continue these notes : he finds the use of *w* for *v* prevalent in Boston and Philadelphia, as *weal* for *veal*, but unknown in Hartford. " Vast numbers of people in Boston and the neighborhood use *w* for *v ;* yet I never once heard this pronunciation in Connecticut." He regards this use as the survival of old custom, but since the nation in general had made a distinction, every person should resign his peculiarities for the sake of uniformity. "The words *either, neither, deceit, conceit, receipt,* are generally pronounced by the Eastern people *ither, nither, desate, consate, resate.* These are errors; all the standard authors agree to give *ei* in these words the sound of *ee.* This is the practice in England, in the Middle and Southern States, and, what is higher authority, analogy warrants the practice." He hesitates between *oblige* and *obleege,* the weight of authority being equally divided, but analogy persuades him to the former. Analogy also requires Európean, though modern fashionable speakers have been introducing the innovation of Européan. "In the Middle and Southern States *fierce, pierce, tierce,* are pronounced *feerce, peerce, teerce.* To convince the people of the impropriety of this pronunciation, it might be sufficient to inform them that it is not fashionable on the English theatre. . . . The standard English pronunciation now is *ferce, perce, terce,* and it is universal in New England." He arraigns the fashionable world for pronouncing *heard* as *herd,* instead of by its true sound of *heard,* in analogy with *feared.* "*Beard* is sometimes, but erroneously, pronounced *beerd*. General practice, both in England and America, requires that *e* should be pronounced as in *were*, and I know of no rule opposed to the practice." He objects to the innovation of *woond* for *wound*, and enters upon a long discussion of the pronunciation of *nature*, finally falling back upon his countrymen's *natur*.

Webster inculcated his views on orthography and pronunciation upon all occasions. He wrote, he lectured, he pressed home his doctrines upon persons and assemblies. He was one of the first to perceive the importance of getting his principles adopted in printing-houses. Long after the time of which I am writing he continued to act as a missionary in philology. The present printer of " Webster's Dictionary " remembers that when he was a boy of thirteen, working at the case in Burlington, Vermont, a little pale-faced man came into the office and handed him a printed slip, saying, " My lad, when you use these words, please oblige me by spelling them as here : *theater*, *center*," etc. It was Noah Webster traveling about among the printing-offices, and

persuading people to spell as he did : a better illustration could not be found of the reformer's sagacity, and his patient method of
effecting his purpose.

His contemporaries were obliged to take
sides when so aggressive a spirit was among
them. His doctrines were discussed in society and in print. The Φ B K Society at
Yale debated upon the adoption of Webster's orthography, deciding in 1792 in favor
of it, and reversing their decision in 1794.
Webster, by the way, was not unmindful of
his college. In 1790, as an encouragement
to the study of the English language, he
made a foundation for an annual prize to be
given to the author of the composition which
should be judged best by the faculty ; but
the foundation does not appear to have been
permanent. Just as later he went to the
printing-offices to secure a conformity to his
orthography, so in the earlier years he had
directed his arguments at the schools. In
1798 he published " A Letter to the Governors, Instructors, and Trustees of the Universities, and other Seminaries of Learning
in the United States, on the Errors of English Grammar," from which I have already

quoted ; and appeals to these men, who are to give direction to the education of the young, to free themselves from a slavish dependence upon England. " It will be honorable to us as a nation, and more useful to our native tongue and to science, that we examine the grounds of all rules and changes before we adopt them, and reject all such as have not obvious propriety for their foundation or utility for their object."

Webster's studies had thus been gravitating toward lexicography, and the habits of mind which had been confirmed in his various pursuits were precisely such as would serve best the purpose which he was gradually forming. Dr. Chauncey Goodrich, in the memoir which is prefixed to the Dictionary, remarks upon certain habits formed by him early in life, which, becoming fixed principles, were of inestimable advantage in his labors afterward. While his memory was tenacious, he was a great hoarder of documents and marker of books ; he was a careful methodizer of his knowledge ; he accustomed himself to a great variety and to unceasing diligence in literary toil, and he was perpetually going back of facts to the principles which he thought to underlie them.

It had been his custom for many years to jot down words which he met in reading, and failed to find in dictionaries, and his labors upon the Spelling-Book and Grammar had familiarized him with the task of discriminating and defining, and had also disclosed to him the deficiencies in that respect of current dictionaries. In 1806 he published "A Compendious Dictionary of the English Language," in which he announced, with an amusing foretaste of the larger claims of the "Unabridged," that it contained five thousand more words than were to be found in the best English compends. The Dictionary was rendered still more useful by taking under its protection various tables of moneys and weights, an official list of all the post-offices in the United States, the number of inhabitants in the several States, and new and instructive chronological tables. This, by the way, was the first occasion, I think, when a word-book had departed from the customary boundaries of such literature. I have been able to find but one precedent, Dyche and Pardon's Dictionary, which, published a few years before, had contained a supplementary list of persons and places, arranged alphabetically, and apparently only as a museum of curiosities. This Dictionary had, however, as a part of its regular text the several market towns in England and Wales, with a general description of the places, their situation, market-days, government, manufacture, number of representatives sent to parliament, and distance from London. The encyclopædic features of a dictionary are clearly of American addition, growing out of the more general and exclusive use of the Dictionary as a book of reference, and increased by the suggestions of competition. The Dictionary proper was an enlargement of Entick, and in this preliminary work Webster exercised very little authority in deviating from the generally accepted orthography. The extent of his changes is indicated in his preface : —

" In a few instances I have preferred the orthography of Newton, Prideaux, Hook, Dryden, Whiston, etc., to that of Johnson, as being more analogical and purely English, as *scepter*, *sepulcher*. In omitting *u*

in *honour* and a few words of that class I
have pursued a common practice in this
country, authorized by the principle of uniformity and by etymology, as well as by
Ash's Dictionary. In omitting *k* after *c* [as
in *public*] I have unequivocal propriety and
the present usage for my authorities. In
a few words, modern writers are gradually
purifying the orthography from its corruptions. Thus, Edwards in his 'History of
the West Indies,' and Gregory in his 'Economy of Nature,' Pope, Hoole, etc., restore
mold to its true spelling; and it would be
no small convenience to revive the etymological spelling of *aker*. Cullen, in his
translation of 'Clavigero,' follows Bacon
and Davenport in the true Saxon orthography of *drouth ;* and the elegant Blackstone
has corrected the orthography of *nusance*
and *duchy*. The diphthongs in words borrowed from the Latin language have gradually been sinking into desuetude for a century; the few which remain I have ex-
punged."

Dr. Johnson was the Magnus Apollo of
lexicographers then, and his bulky fame
still casts a large shadow over the world of

words. To rebel against his autocratic rule at the beginning of this century was to write one's self down an audacious and presuming sciolist. It is not surprising, therefore, that Webster's criticism of Johnson in this Dictionary and in other places should have exposed him to censure. Dr. Ramsay of Charleston, a man of consequence in his day, wrote him that the " prejudices against any American attempts to improve Dr. Johnson were very strong in that city." The letter gave Webster his opportunity, and he at once wrote and published his vigorous pamphlet respecting the " Errors in Johnson's Dictionary and other Lexicons," which is addressed to Dr. Ramsay. He takes a very lofty view of the situation. " The intelligence," he writes, of this resentment in Charleston, " is not wholly unexpected, for similar prejudices have been manifested in some parts of the Northern States. A man who has read with slight attention the history of nations, in their advances from barbarism to civilization and science, cannot be surprised at the strength of prejudices long established and never disturbed. Few centuries have elapsed since many men lost

their lives or their liberty by publishing
NEW TRUTHS ; and not two centuries have
past since Galileo was imprisoned by an
ecclesiastical court, for defending the truth
of the Copernican System, condemned to do
penance for three years, and his book burnt
at Rome, as containing dangerous and dam-
nable heresies. This example is cited as
one of a multitude which the history of man
presents to our view ; and if it differs in *degree*, it accords in *principle*, with the case
now before the American public."

He then, after admitting the value of
Johnson's ethical writings, but distrusting
his philological attainments, makes good his
objections by detailed specifications. He
condemns the insertion of a multitude of
words which do not belong to the language,
mentioning such unnaturalized foreigners
as *adversable, advesperate, adjugate, agricu-
lation, abstrude, injudicable, spicosity, crap-
ulence, morigerous, tenebrosity, balbucinate,
illachrymable*, etc., words to which the
reader may, if he knows Latin, attach some
sort of meaning, but which he would be
slow to introduce into his speech or writing. Then he condemns Johnson's reference

to writers of the seventeenth century who buried their thoughts beneath cumbrous piles of Latinized English, as in such passages as : —

" The intire or broken *compagination* of the magnetical fabric; " " The effects of their activity are not precipitously *abrupted*, but gradually proceed to their cessations;" "Some have written rhetorically and *concessively*, not controverting, but assuming, the question, which, taken as granted, advantaged the illation; " " Its fluctuations are but motions subservient, which winds, shelves, and every interjacency *irregulates ;* " passages given as illustrative of the words italicized. " From a careful examination of this work, and its effect upon the language, I am inclined to believe that Johnson's authority has multiplied instead of reducing the number of corruptions in the English language. Let any man of correct taste cast his eye on such words as *denominable, opiniatry, ariolation, assation, ataraxy, clancular, comminuible, conclusible, dedentition, deuteroscopy, digladiation, dignotion, cubiculary, discubitory, exolution, exeuterate, incompossible, incompossibility,*

indigitate, etc., and let him say whether a
dictionary which gives thousands of such
terms as authorized English words is a safe
standard of writing. . . . In the ' English-
Dutch Dictionary' of Willcocke, we find the
compiler has translated *ariolation, clancular,
denomiable, comminuible*, etc., into Dutch.
In Bailey's ' Fahrenkruger,' we see *digladiation, dignotion, exeuterate*, etc., turned into
German. These, or similar words, are by
Neuman translated into Spanish, and where
the mischief ends it is impossible to ascer-
tain. And what must foreigners think of
English taste and erudition, when they are
told that their dictionaries contain thousands of such words which are not used by
the English nation ! "

Webster's next point is that Johnson has
exceeded the bounds of legitimate lexicography by the admission of vulgar and cant
words. "It may be alleged that it is the
duty of a lexicographer to insert and define
all words found in English books : then
such words as *fishify, jackalent, parma-city,
jiggumbob, conjobble, foutra*, etc., are legitimate English words ! Alas, had a native
of the United States introduced such vulgar

words and offensive ribaldry into a similar work, what columns of abuse would have issued from the Johnsonian presses against the wretch who could thus sully his book and corrupt the language!" He criticises the accuracy with which Johnson has discriminated the different senses of the same word, and words nearly synonymous. The illustrative quotations which bear so much of the praise bestowed upon Johnson's Dictionary he declares to be one of the most exceptionable features, both because no small number of the examples are taken from authors who did not write the language with purity, and because a still larger number throw no light upon the definitions, and are frequently entirely unnecessary. He cites on this last point the passages under the word *alley*, five in all, from Spenser, Bacon, Milton, Dryden, and Pope. " Does any reader of English want all these authorities to show the word to be legitimate? Far from it, nineteen twentieths of all our words are so common that they require no proof at all of legitimacy. Yet the example here given is by no means the most exceptionable for the number of authorities cited. The author sometimes offers thirty or forty lines to illustrate words which every man, woman, and child understands as well as Johnson. Thirty-five lines of exemplification under the word *froth*, for example, are just as useless in explaining the word as would be the same number of lines from the language of the Six Nations."

His final charge rests on the inaccuracy of the etymology. " As this has been generally considered the least important part of a dictionary the subject has been little investigated, and is very imperfectly understood, even by men of science. Johnson scarcely entered the threshold of the subject. He consulted chiefly Junius and Skinner; the latter of whom was not possessed of learning adequate to the investigation, and Junius, like Vossius, Scaliger, and most other etymologists on the Continent, labored to deduce all languages from the Greek. Hence these authors neglected the principal sources of information, which were to be found only in the north of Europe, and in the west of Ireland and Scotland. In another particular they all failed of success; they never discovered some of the principal modes in which the primitive radical words were combined to form the more modern compounds. On this subject, therefore, almost *everything remains to be done.* . . . I can assure the American public that the errors in Johnson's Dictionary are ten times as numerous as they suppose; and that the confidence now reposed in its accuracy is the greatest injury to philology that now exists. I can assure them further that if any man, whatever may be his abilities in other respects, should attempt to compile a new dictionary, or amend Johnson's, without a profound knowledge of etymology, he will unquestionably do as much harm as good."

A few years later Webster found an opportunity to attack the general subject of lexicography from another side, and one intimately connected with his special work. In 1816 Hon. John Pickering published "A Vocabulary, or Collection of Words and Phrases which have been supposed to be peculiar to the United States of America. To which is prefixed an Essay on the Present State of the English Language in the United States;" he had cited Webster upon various words and plainly was aiming

15

at him in his preface, when he declared that
"in this country, as in England, we have
thirsty reformers and presumptuous sciolists, who would unsettle the whole of our
admirable language, for the purpose of making it conform to their whimsical notions of
propriety." Webster at once addressed a
letter in print to Pickering, and took up
weapons, offensive and defensive, with alacrity and confidence.

"This is a heavy accusation, Sir, from a
gentleman of your talents, liberality, and
candor," he writes. "Sciolists we may
have in multitudes; but who are the men
who would unsettle the whole of our language? Can you name the men, or any of
them, either in this country or in England?
Surely the finger of scorn ought to be
pointed at the men who are base enough
to wish, and sottish enough to attempt, to
unsettle a whole language. I am confident,
Sir, that deliberate reflection will induce
you to retract a charge so injurious to your
fellow-citizens. It certainly becomes you,
and the character you maintain in society,
to learn the distinction between an attempt
to find what the language is, and an attempt

to unsettle its principles. Whether you
number me with the thirsty reformers and
presumptuous sciolists is a fact which I shall
take no pains to discover, nor, if known,
would the fact give me the smallest concern." Webster's hand trembles evidently
with suppressed anger, but he grows firmer
as he goes on. " My studies have been
sometimes directed to philology, for the
exclusive purpose of ascertaining and un-
folding its principles, correcting abuses, and
supplying the defect of rules in our elementary treatises. In the course of my researches I have discovered a multitude of
errors and false principles, and numerous
defects in such treatises; and as I have
pushed my inquiries probably much farther
than any other man, I am satisfied that the
evidence I can lay before the public will
convince you that there is a rich mine of
knowledge to be opened on this subject
that your English friends have never yet
discovered." He takes up Pickering's Vocabulary and rapidly criticises the several
entries; he renews his criticism upon Johnson and Lowth, but the most interesting
part of the pamphlet is his stout advocacy

of the claim of Americans to make and accept changes of language which grow out of their own conditions. The English language was a common inheritance in England and America, and in the necessary growth of a spoken language, Americans had equal right with Englishmen to contribute to the growth; nay, that the American was not a dialect of the English, but a variation; not a departure from a standard existing in contemporary England, but an independent branch from a common stock.

"New words should not be introduced into a copious language without reason, nor contrary to its analogies. But a living language must keep pace with improvements in knowledge, and with the multiplication of ideas. Those who would entirely restrain the practice of using new words seem not to consider that the limit they now prescribe would have been as just and rational, a thousand or two thousand years ago, as it is at this period. If it should be said, we have words enough to express all our ideas, it may be truly answered, so had our ancestors when they left the plains of Germany; or when they first crossed the Hellespont;

or when they left the soil of Persia. And what then? Would the words they then used be now sufficient for our purpose. And who can define the bounds of future improvement? Who will venture to allege that men have not yet as much to learn as they have already learnt? The smallest acquaintance with the history of human society and improvement ought to silence the critics on this subject.

" Nor are we to believe that two nations inhabiting countries separated by a wide ocean can preserve a perfect uniformity of language. If a perfect uniformity cannot be produced or preserved in two distant counties in England, how is this object to be effected between the English in Great Britain and their descendants in America, India, or New Holland? Let history answer the question. The art of printing, interchange of books, and commercial intercourse will retard the progress of mutation and diversities; but no human means can prevent some changes, and the adaptation of language to diversities of condition and improvement. The process of a living language is like the motion of a broad river, which flows with a slow, silent, irresistible current." He turns the tables on a writer who points out American barbarisms by showing a number of English barbarisms which had been creeping into use, and declares that in the use of language one nation as well as the other will commit these errors, but he returns again and again to his position that Americans in their use of language are not to wait passively upon English authority.

"I venerate," he says, "the men and their writings ; I venerate the literature, the laws, the institutions, and the charities of the land of my fathers. But I deprecate the effects of a blind acquiescence in the opinions of men, and the passive reception of everything that comes from a foreign press. My mind revolts at the reverence for foreign authors, which stifles inquiry, restrains investigation, benumbs the vigor of the intellectual faculties, subdues and debases the mind. I regret to see the young Hercules of genius in America chained to his cradle. . . . I left college with the same veneration for English writers, and the same confidence in their opinions, which most of my countrymen now possess, and I adopted their errors without examination. After many years of research, I am compelled to withdraw much of that confidence, and to look with astonishment upon the errors and false principles which they have propagated; some of them of far more consequence than any which have been mentioned in the preceding remarks. I wish to be on good terms with the English; it is my interest and the interest of my fellow-citizens to treat them as friends and brethren. But I will be neither frowned nor ridiculed into error, and a servile imitation of practices which I know or believe to be corrupt. I will examine subjects for myself, and endeavor to find the truth, and to defend it, whether it accords with English opinions or not. If I must measure swords with their travelers and their reviewers, on the subject under consideration, I shall not decline the combat. There is nothing which, in my opinion, so debases the genius and character of my countrymen as the implicit confidence they place in English authors, and their unhesitating submission to their opinions, their derision, and their frowns. But I trust the time will come when the English will be convinced that the intellectual faculties of their descendants have not degenerated in America; and that we can contend with them in LETTERS with as much success as upon the OCEAN.

"I am not ignorant, Sir, of the narrowness of the sphere which I now occupy. Secluded, in a great measure, from the world, with small means, and no adventitious aid from men of science; with little patronage to extend my influence, and powerful enmities to circumscribe it; what can my efforts avail in attempting to counteract a current of opinion? Yet I am not accustomed to despondence. I have contributed in a small degree to the instruction of at least four millions of the rising generation; and it is not unreasonable to expect that a few seeds of improvement, planted by my hand, may germinate and grow and ripen into valuable fruit, when my remains shall be mingled with the dust." A note is added, in which Webster with grave banter offers a suit of clothes to any English or American reviewer who will find a man capable of explaining the little word *by*, stating its primary signification and its true sense in its several uses and applications.

The spirit with which Webster defended himself was a manly one, and it is noticeable how years of fencing had improved the temper of his weapons. He was keener in his thrusts, more dexterous and supple, and comported himself in these disputes as a man entirely confident of his position. It is not vanity which upholds a man working silently year after year at a task ridiculed by his neighbors and denounced by his enemies. Webster had something better to sustain him than an idle self-conceit. He had the reserve of a high purpose, and an aim which had been growing more clearly understood by himself, so that he could afford to disregard the judgments of others. There was in the outward circumstance of his life something which testifies to the sincerity and worth of his purpose. He had withdrawn himself into the wilderness that he might free himself from encumbrances in his work, and with his love of society this was no light thing to do. His family went with him reluctantly; but when did not an enthusiast drag with him to his own light sacrifice the unwilling attendants of his life!

CHAPTER VII.

AN AMERICAN DICTIONARY OF THE ENG-
LISH LANGUAGE.

AT the close of the Preface to his Compendious Dictionary, Webster announced his intention of compiling and publishing a full and comprehensive dictionary of the language. After answering the objections which candid friends might raise, he added: " From a different class of men, if such are to be found, whose criticism would sink the literature of this country even lower than the distorted representations of foreign reviewers, — whose veneration for transatlantic authors leads them to hold American writers in unmerited contempt, — from such men I neither expect nor solicit favor. However arduous the task, and however feeble my powers of body and mind, a thorough conviction of the necessity and importance of the undertaking has overcome my fears and objections, and determined me to make an effort to dissipate the charm of veneration for foreign authors which fascinates the minds of men in this country and holds them in the chains of illusion. In the investigation of this subject great labor is to be sustained, and numberless difficulties encountered; but with a humble dependence on Divine favor for the preservation of my life and health, I shall prosecute the work with diligence, and execute it with a fidelity suited to its importance."

It was 1806 when he sat down to the task, and twenty years of almost continuous labor were expended before the work then projected was given to the world in the first edition of the "American Dictionary of the English Language," in two volumes quarto. Complete absorption in his work, which could yield nothing until it was completed, crippled his resources, confined now in the main to copyright from his Spelling-Book; and in 1812 he removed, as we have already seen, for economy's sake, from New Haven to Amherst. During the next ten years he nearly completed the bulk of the Dictionary, but there still remained much to do in the way of comparison and finer study than his own library afforded. He returned to New Haven in 1822, but further work there showed the insufficiency of material to be had in America; and in 1824, leaving his family, he took with him a son and set out for Europe, for the purpose of consulting men and books. He spent two months in Paris, where S. G. Goodrich met him. "A slender form, with a black coat, black small-clothes, black silk stockings, moving back and forth, with its hands behind it, and evidently in a state of meditation. It was a curious, quaint, Connecticut-looking apparition, strangely in contrast to the prevailing forms and aspects in this gay metropolis. I said to myself, 'If it were possible, I should say that was Noah Webster!' I went up to him and found it was indeed he."

He was satisfied that he should work to better advantage in England. He went accordingly to Cambridge in the early fall of 1824, and remained there until the following May, using the resources of the University, and making such connections as he could, though he found rather barren sympathy from English scholars, and small encouragement from English publishers. His training and studies, moreover, were not such as to place him in very cordial relationship with Englishmen, and his attitude toward the scholastic deposit of an old nation may be guessed from a passage in one of his letters home, in which he writes : " The colleges are mostly old stone buildings, which look very heavy, cold, and gloomy to an American accustomed to the new public buildings in our country."

There is something in the whole undertaking, and in the mode of its execution, which makes one by turns wonder at the splendid will and undaunted perseverance of this Yankee teacher, and feel a well-bred annoyance at his blindness to the incongruous position which he occupied. One is disposed to laugh sardonically over this self-taught dictionary-maker, encamped at Cambridge, coolly pursuing his work of an American Dictionary of the English Language in the midst of all that traditional scholarship. But Webster's own consciousness was of the gravity of his work. " When I finished my copy," he writes in a letter to Dr. Thomas Miner, " I was sitting at my table in Cambridge, England, January, 1825. When I arrived at the last word I was seized with a tremor that made it difficult to proceed. I, however, summoned up strength to finish the work, and then, walking about the room, I soon recovered." This may be a faint echo of Gibbon's celebrated passage, but it is inherently truthful, and marks the effect upon him of a sustained purpose, brought, after a score of years, to completion. The Dictionary was published three years after his return to America, and passed through one revision at Mr. Webster's hands in 1840. He was still at work upon it when he died, in 1843. It is fair to look to the preface of a great work, especially of one which seems to admit little personality, for an account of the motives and aims of the workman. In following the lines of Webster's preface we discover the principles which we have already noted stated anew and with increasing confidence. He gives reasons why it had become necessary that an English dictionary should be revised to meet the exigencies of American as distinct from English life, and he says finally: "One consideration, however, which

is dictated by my own feelings, but which I
trust will meet with approbation in corre-
spondent feelings in my fellow-citizens, ought
not to be passed in silence ; it is this : ' The
chief glory of a nation,' says Dr. Johnson,
' arises from its authors.' With this opinion deeply impressed on my mind, I have
the same ambition which actuated that great
man when he expressed a wish to give celebrity to Bacon, to Hooker, to Milton, and
to Boyle. I do not, indeed, expect to add
celebrity to the names of Franklin, Washington, Adams, Jay, Madison, Marshall,
Ramsay, Dwight, Smith, Trumbull, Hamilton, Belknap, Ames, Mason, Kent, Hare,
Silliman, Cleaveland, Walsh, Irving, and
many other Americans distinguished by
their writings or by their science ; but it is
with pride and satisfaction that I can place
them, as authorities, on the same page with
those of Boyle, Hooker, Milton, Dryden,
Addison, Ray, Milner, Cowper, Thomson,
Davy, and Jameson. A life devoted to reading and to an investigation of the origin and
principles of our vernacular language, and
especially a particular examination of the
best English writers, with a view to a com-

parison of their style and phraseology with those of the best American writers and with our colloquial usage, enables me to affirm, with confidence, that the genuine English idiom is as well preserved by the unmixed English of this country as it is by the best *English* writers. Examples to prove this fact will be found in the Introduction to this work. It is true that many of our writers have neglected to cultivate taste and the embellishments of style, but even these have written the language in its genuine *idiom*. In this respect Franklin and Washington, whose language is their hereditary mother-tongue, unsophisticated by modern grammar, present as pure models of genuine English as Addison and Swift. But I may go further, and affirm with truth that our country has produced some of the best models of composition. The style of President Smith, of the authors of the Federalist, of Mr. Ames, of Dr. Mason, of Mr. Harper, of Chancellor Kent, [the prose]" happily bracketed reservation! "of Mr. Barlow, of Dr. Channing, of Washington Irving, of the legal decisions of the Supreme Court of the United States, of the reports of legal decis-

16

ions in some of the particular States, and many other writings, in purity, in elegance, and in technical precision, is equalled only by that of the best British authors, and surpassed by that of no English compositions of a similar kind.

" The United States commenced their existence under circumstances wholly novel and unexampled in the history of nations. They commenced with civilization, with learning, with science, with constitutions of free government, and with that best gift of God to man, the Christian religion. Their population is now equal to that of England; in arts and sciences our citizens are very little behind the most enlightened people on earth, — in some respects they have no superiors; and our language within two centuries will be spoken by more people in this country than any language on earth, except the Chinese, in Asia, and even that may not be an exception."

It is instructive to compare the preface with the celebrated one by Dr. Johnson, introducing his dictionary. Webster, filled with a parochial enthusiasm for his native country, exaggerates the necessity for a

local dictionary, and anticipates the vast
audience that will one day require his work.
To him language is the instrument not so
much of literature as of daily association.
He thinks of a dictionary as a book of reference for the plain reader, and a guide
to him in the correct use of his vernacular. Johnson, proud of his literary heri-
tage, burdened with a sense of his own in-
adequacy, at once confesses the dignity of
his work and the melancholy of his own
nature. He acknowledges the limitation of
his own philological attainments, and rests
his claims to honor upon the fullness with
which he has gathered and arranged the
materials scattered through the vast area of
English literature. The one sees the subject from the side of nationality, the other
from that of literature. Webster is thinking of his own people, Johnson of the un-
national tribe of scholars and men of letters.
The historical associations justify each, for
Johnson was distinctly the member of a
great class which was beginning to assert
its independence of social authority. With
all his loyalty to his king, he was at heart a
republican in literature, and stoutly denied

the divine right of patrons. His dictionary
was the sign of literary emancipation ; it
was the witness to an intellectual freedom
which might be in alliance with government, but could not be its tool. The history of English literature since that date is
a democratic history. Webster, on his part,
was the prophet of a national independence,
in which language and literature were involved as inseparable elements. To him
books were neither the production nor the
possession of a class, but necessarily incident to the life of a free people. Hence, in
his citation of American authorities, he is
undaunted by the paucity of purely literary men ; law reports and state documents
answer his purpose as well. He saw literature as the accompaniment of self-government, and the dictionary in his eyes was a
vast school-book, not a thesaurus of literature.

I can hardly expect my readers to follow
me patiently through a close examination of
the successive editions of Webster's large
dictionary, and I have no such high opinion
of my own patience as to suppose that I
should continue on the road after my read-

ers had dropped behind ; but it is possible to make a rough comparison of the first edition of 1828 and the latest of 1880, in order to see what Webster did which needed . to be undone, and to form some estimate of the substantial service which he rendered lexicography in that edition which was more nearly his sole and unaided work.

To take, then, the matter of orthography, there are certain general classes of words which have borne the brunt of criticism. In his first edition Webster's rule was to omit *k* after *c* from the end of all words of more than one syllable, and to retain it in longer forms of the same word only when it was required to defend the hard sound of *c*. He wrote thus : *public*, *publication*. But Webster, like writers of to-day, was constantly allowing his uniform rule to give way in cases where custom had fastened upon him. Thus he still spelled *traffick*, *almanack*, *frolick*, *havock*, and it was quite possible for his critics to follow him through a long list of words of this class and detect his frequent aberration from a uniform rule. Yet, instead of receding from his position, the latest edition advances ; a nicer discrimination is made in the etymological origin of the variation, but in point of practice a much more general conformity to the rule is recorded. There can be no question that the *k* has a foreign air when found in such cases in American books.

Again, Webster omitted the *u* in the unaccented termination *our*, as *honor* for *honour*. In this, too, he was not without English precedent. Johnson was singularly inconsistent in this respect, and his influence has extended over English orthography to the present day, so that one cannot take up a well-printed English journal without discovering an apparently arbitrary use of the termination. The usage as recorded by Webster has held its ground, and there is no variation between the first and latest editions, except that the alternative form *Saviour* is given in the latest as a concession to an undefined sense of sanctity which would lead to a separation of the word from its class. There is a foot-note in the edition of 1828, in which Washington's omission of *u* is cited as an argument in favor of the form *or*.

There is the vexed form *er* for *re* in such

words as *center* for *centre*. It is fair on this
point to give the note which Webster originally made in defense of his position: " A
similar fate has attended the attempt to An-
glicize the orthography of another class of
words, which we have received from the
French. At a very early period the words
*chambre, desastre, desordre, chartre, monstre,
tendre, tigre, entre, fievre, diametre, arbitre,
nombre,* and others were reduced to the English form of spelling: *chamber, disaster,
charter, monster, tender, tiger, enter, fever,
diameter, arbiter, number.* At a later period, Sir Isaac Newton, Camden, Selden,
Milton, Whitaker, Prideaux, Hook, Whiston, Bryant, and other authors of the first
character attempted to carry through this
reformation, writing *scepter, center, sepulcher.* But this improvement was arrested,
and a few words of this class retain their
French orthography: such as *metre, mitre,
nitre, spectre, sceptre, theatre, sepulchre,* and
sometimes *centre.* It is remarkable that a
nation distinguished for erudition should
thus reject improvements, and retain anom-
alies, in opposition to all the convenience of
uniformity. I am glad that so respectable a

writer as Mitford has discarded this innovation, and uniformly written *center*, *scep-*
ter, *theater*, *sepulcher*. In the present instance want of uniformity is not the only
evil. The present orthography has introduced an awkward mode of writing the derivatives, for example, *centred*, *sceptred*,
sepulchred; whereas Milton and Pope wrote
these words as regular derivatives of *center*,
scepter, *sepulcher*, thus, ' *Sceptered* king.'
So Coxe in his travels, ' The principal
wealth of the church is *centered* in the
monasteries.' This is correct."

The two Websters agree in the main, but
some of the variations in the first disappear
in the latest. Thus Noah Webster gave
the alternative forms *massacer*, *massacre*,
preferring the former, and *aker*, *acre*, a curious inconsistency ; the editors of the latest
edition have dropped these proposed improvements, and have given secondary alternative forms in *theatre*, *metre*, *centre*,
sepulchre, *nitre*, and perhaps some others.
Both accept *chancre*, *lucre*, and *ogre*. It
may be said in general that the game on
these words is a drawn one, with a stubborn
retention of the *re* form on the part of the

most careful writers, and a growing majority in numbers in favor of the *er* form.

In the edition of 1828 Webster laid down
the rule that verbs ending in a single consonant, but having the accent on the first
syllable, or on a syllable preceding the last,
ought not to double the final consonant in
the derivatives. Thus he wrote *travel*,
traveler, traveling. The editors of the latest
edition find no occasion to revise this rule,
and report that other lexicographers advise
a conformity to it, but they record a large
number of exceptions to satisfy " the prejudice of the eye." His corresponding rule
is " that monosyllabic verbs, ending in a
single consonant, not preceded by a long
vowel, and other verbs ending in a single
accented consonant, and of course not preceded by a long vowel, double the final consonant in all the derivatives which are
formed by a termination beginning with a
vowel." This applies to *fit, fitted, compel,
compelled*. This rule, like the other, is retained by the later editors, though both rules
are more exactly framed. No question has
been raised upon this point, and the nice
correspondence of the two rules is likely in

process of time to break down those exceptions to the former which usage now makes familiar.

Does the reader, when he writes, hesitate perilously before the words *distil* or *distill, control* or *controll, recal* or *recall?* It can only be said that neither Webster nor his editors could frame a rule which they were ready to follow. They agree in their inconsistencies, and have brought over other lexicographers in some cases to their disposition to double the *l.* The indecision, however, which one feels before *skilful* or *skillful* is more painful, — are we to say *painfull?* Here again the first and latest editions of Webster are at one with each other, and at variance with old and established usage. The editors of Webster appear to yield the ground a little by conceding that *skilful, dulness,* and like words are so written by many. Webster's change in this respect seems therefore to have made no headway except in his own family.

There are other words which may be grouped in classes, but I will content myself with a further enumeration, somewhat at random, of words which Webster trifled with, as his enemies might say, or reduced to order, as he would claim; placing in parallel columns the spelling adopted in the first edition and that followed in the latest : —

Edition of 1828.	Edition of 1880.
ax	ax } axe
controller	comptroller } controller
contemporary	contemporary } cotemporary
defense	defense } defence
ambassador	embassador } ambassador
gantlet } gauntlet	gantlet } gauntlet
drouth	drought
group } groop	group
height } heighth } hight	height } hight
maneuver	maneuver } manœuvre
melasses	molasses
mold	mold } mould
molt	molt } moult
plow	plow } plough

tongue } tung }	tongue
wo	woe
crum	crumb
pontif	pontiff
ake } ache }	ache
maiz	maize
gimblet	gimlet
feather } fether }	feather
steady } steddy }	steady
mosk	mosque
ribin	ribbon
cutlas	cutlass
skain	skain } skein }
sherif	sheriff
porpess	porpoise

It should be added that in many cases where the later editors have receded from Webster's advanced position they have added a note approving his innovation as etymologically correct and preferable. There can be no doubt that Webster was careless and inconsistent in his entry of these words, since he would venture his improvement under the word, fling scorn at the current usage, and then, when using the word elsewhere in definition or in compounds, forget his improvement and follow the customary orthography. From our rapid survey of the orthography, however, it may be said in general that Webster's decision in the case of classes of words has been maintained in subsequent editions, but his individual alterations have been regarded as contributions to an impossibly ideal correct orthography, and quietly dropped. The fact illustrates Webster's strength and weakness. His notions on the subject of uniformity were often very sensible, and he had the advantage of reducing to order what was hopelessly chaotic in common usage. But his sense of the stability of usage was imperfect, and when he moved among the words at random, arranging the language to suit his personal taste, he discovered or his successors did that words have roots of another kind than what etymologists regard.

Webster was wont to defend himself against the common charge of proposing new forms of words, by showing that, if one went far enough back, he would be sure to come upon the same forms in English lit-

erature ; that his aim was to restore, not to
invent, and to bring back the language to
its earlier and historic shape.   This is a defense familiar to us in these later days of
spelling reform ; and no one doubts, who
knows the chaos of English spelling before
the days of printing, that authority could
be found for any favorite mode of spelling
a word.   Webster claimed the same conservative principles in the matter of pronunciation, and stoutly declared that he was
a champion for historic English sounds as
opposed to the innovations offered by Sheridan, Walker, and Jamieson.   "The language of a nation," he says in his Introduction, " is the common property of the people,
and no individual has a right to make in-
roads upon its principles.   As it is the me-

dium of communication between men, it is
important that the same written words and
the same oral sounds to express the same
ideas should be used by the whole nation.
When any man, therefore, attempts to
change the established orthography or pronunciation, except to correct palpable errors
and produce uniformity by recalling wan-
derers into the pale of regular analogies, he

offers an indignity to the nation. No local practice, however respectable, will justify the attempt. There is great dignity, as well as propriety, in respecting the universal and long-established usages of a nation. With these views of the subject, I feel myself bound to reject all modern innovations which violate the established principles and analogies of the language, and destroy or impair the value of alphabetical writing. I have therefore endeavored to present to my fellow-citizens the English language in its genuine purity, as we have received the inheritance from our ancestors, without removing a landmark. If the language is fatally destined to be corrupted, I will not be an instrument of the mischief."

These are certainly brave words, and there are even people who would doubt if Webster had the courage of such convictions. In his Dictionary he seems to have somewhat underestimated the importance of noting the pronunciation. He devotes a number of pages, it is true, in the Introduction, to a discussion of the principles involved, but in marking the words he used only the simplest method, and disregarded refinements of

speech. The word culture, for instance, is
marked by him ɛul'ture, while in the latest
edition it appears as ɛŭlt'ūre (kŭlt'yụr). He
had a few antipathies, as to the *tsh* sound
then fashionable in such words as *tumult,* and
with a certain native pugnacity he attacked
the orthoepists who at that time had elabo-
rated their system more than had the orthog-
raphists; he did not believe that nice shades
of sound could be represented to the eye by
characters, and he appears to have been
somewhat impatient of the whole subject.
He maintained that the speech which generally prevailed in New England in his day
represented the best and most historic pronunciation. The first ministers had been
educated at the universities, and the respect
felt for them had led to a general accept-
ance of their mode of speech. He himself
said *vollum* for volume, and *pătriot,* and
perce for pierce. He regarded Sheridan,
Walker, Perry, Jones, and Jamieson as having, in their attempts at securing uniformity,
only unsettled the old and familiar speech,
— a curious commentary on his own performances in orthography. He does not
here, either, forget his loyalty to America.

" In a few instances," he says, " the common usage of a great and respectable portion of the people of this country accords with the analogies of the language, but not with the modern notation of English orthoepists. In such cases it seems expedient and proper to retain our own usage. To renounce a practice confessedly regular for one confessedly anomalous, out of respect to foreign usage, would hardly be consistent with the dignity of lexicography. When we have principle on our side, let us adhere to it. The time cannot be distant when the population of this vast country will throw off their leading-strings, and walk in their own strength ; and the more we can raise the credit and authority of principle over the caprices of fashion and innovation, the nearer we approach to uniformity and stability of practice."

The absence of the finer qualities of scholarship in Webster's composition is indicated by his somewhat rough and ready treatment of the subject of pronunciation ; perhaps no more delicate test exists of the grain of an educated person's culture than that of pronunciation It is far more subtle

than orthography or grammar, and pleasure
in conversation, when analyzed, will show
this fine sense of sound and articulation to
be the last element.

If any one had asked Webster upon what
part of his Dictionary he had expended the
most time and now set the highest value, he
would undoubtedly have answered at once
the etymology, and whatever related to
the history and derivation of words. The
greater part of the time given continuously,
from 1807 to 1826, to the elaboration of his
Dictionary was spent upon this department;
his severest condemnation of Johnson was
upon the score of his ignorance in these par-
ticulars, and the credit which he took to
himself was frank and sincere. There can
be no doubt that he worked hard; there can
be no doubt, either, that he had his way to
make almost unaided by previous explorers.
The science of comparative philology is of
later birth; the English of Webster's day
were no better equipped than he for the
task which he undertook, except so far as
they were trained by scholarship to avoid
an empirical method. Horne Tooke was
the man who opened Webster's eyes, and

him he followed so long as he followed anybody. But Tooke was a guesser, and Webster, with all his deficiencies, had always a strong reliance upon system and method. He made guesses also, but he thought they were scientific analyses, and he came to the edge of real discoveries without knowing it.

The fundamental weakness of Webster's work in etymology lay in his reliance upon external likenesses and the limitation of his knowledge to mere vocabularies. It was not an idle pedantry which made him marshal an imposing array of words from Oriental languages; he was on the right track when he sought for a common ground upon which Indo-European languages could meet, but he lacked that essential knowledge of grammatical forms, without which a knowledge of the vocabulary is liable to be misleading. His comparison of languages may be compared to the earlier labors of students in comparative anatomy who mistook merely external resemblances for structural homology. It would be idle to institute any inquiry into the agreement of the 1828 edition with the latest edition. All of Webster's original work, as he regarded it, has been swept away, and the etymology reconstructed by Dr. Mahn, of Berlin, in accordance with a science which did not exist in Webster's day. The immense labor which Webster expended remains only as a witness to that indomitable spirit which enabled him to keep steadfastly to his self-imposed task through years of isolation.

The definitions in Webster's first edition offer an almost endless opportunity for comment. He found Johnson's definitions wanting in exactness, and often rather explanations than definitions. For his part he aimed at a somewhat plainer work. He was under no temptation, as Johnson was, to use a fine style, but was rather disposed to take another direction and use an excessive plainness of speech, amplifying his definition by a reference in detail to the synonymous words. It must be said, however, that Webster was often unnecessarily rambling in his account of a word, as when, for instance, under the word *magnanimity* he writes : " Greatness of mind ; that elevation or dignity of soul which encounters danger and trouble with tranquillity and firmness, which raises the possessor above revenge, and makes him delight in acts of benevolence, — which makes him disdain injustice and meanness, and prompts him to sacrifice personal ease, interest, and safety for the accomplishment of useful and noble objects; " in the latest Webster the same terms are used but with a judicious compression. Johnson's account reads, "Greatness of mind; bravery; elevation of soul." Webster was disposed also to mingle rather more encyclopædic information with his definitions than a severer judgment of the limits of a dictionary now permits. Thus under the word *bishop*, besides illustrative passages, he gives at length the mode of election in the English Church, and also that used in the Episcopal Church in America. But this fullness of description was often a positive addition. Here again a comparison may be made with Johnson. Under the word *telescope*, Johnson simply says : " A long glass by which distant objects are viewed." Webster : " An optical instrument employed in viewing distant objects, as the heavenly bodies. It assists the eye chiefly in two ways : first, by enlarging the visual angle

under which a distant object is seen, and
thus magnifying that object; and secondly,
by collecting and conveying to the eye a
larger beam of light than would enter the
naked organ, and thus rendering objects distinct and visible which would otherwise be
indistinct and invisible. Its essential parts
are the *object-glass*, which collects the beams
of light and forms an image of the object, and
the *eyeglass*, which is a microscope by which
the image is magnified." The latest editors
have found nothing to change in this definition and nothing to add, except a long account of the several kinds of telescopes. In
the introduction and the definition of words
employed in science Webster was for the
time in advance of Johnson, as the present
Webster is far in advance of the first from
the natural increase in the importance and
number of these terms. But Webster did
not merely use his advantages; he had a
keener sense than Johnson of the relative
weight of such words. Johnson harbored
them as unliterary, but Webster welcomed
them as a part of the growing vocabulary
of the people.

Webster claimed to have nearly doubled

the number of words given in Johnson, even after he had excluded a number which found their place in Johnson. He swelled the list, it is true, by the use of compounds under *un* and similar prefixes, but the noticeable fact remains that he incorporated in the Dictionary a vast number of words which previously had led a private and secluded life in special word-books. His object being to make a dictionary for the American people, his ambition was to produce a book which should render all other books of its class unnecessary. Webster himself enumerates the words added in his Dictionary under five heads: —

1. Words of common use, among which he notes: grand-jury, grand-juror, eulogist, consignee, consignor, mammoth, maltreatment, iceberg, parachute, malpractice, fracas, entailment, perfectibility, glacier, firewarden, safety-valve, savings-bank, gaseous, lithographic, peninsular, repealable, retaliatory, dyspeptic, missionary, nervine, meteoric, mineralogical, reimbursable; to quarantine, revolutionize, retort, patent, explode, electioneer, reorganize, magnetize.

2. Participles of verbs, previously omitted, and often having an adjective value.

3. Terms of frequent occurrence in historical works, especially those derived from proper names, such as Shemitic, Augustan, Gregorian.

4. Legal terms.

5. Terms in the arts and sciences. This was then the largest storehouse, as it has since been, and the reader may be reminded that this great start in lexicography was coincident with the beginning of modern scientific research.

The greatest interest, however, which Webster's vocabulary has for us is in its justification of the title to his Dictionary. It was an American Dictionary, and no one who examines it attentively can fail to perceive how unmistakably it grounds itself on American use. Webster had had an American education ; he made his dictionary for the American people, and as in orthography and pronunciation he followed a usage which was mainly American, in his words and definitions he knew no authority beyond the usage of his own country. Webster's Dictionary of 1807 had already furnished Pickering with a large number of words for his vocabulary of supposed Americanisms, and Webster had replied, defending the words against the charge of corruption ; the Dictionary of 1828 would have supplied many more of the same class. The Americanism, as an English scholar of that day would have judged it, was either in the word itself or in some special application of it. Webster, like many later writers, pointed out that words which had their origin in English local use had here simply become of general service, owing to the freedom of movement amongst the people and the constant tendency toward uniformity of speech. The subject has been carefully treated, and it is unnecessary to consider it here. Enough for us to remember that Webster was not singling out words as Americanisms, but incorporating in the general language all these terms, and calling the record of entire product an American Dictionary of the English Language. The reader may be entertained by a selection of these words and definitions, taken somewhat at random from the vast number of undiscriminated words in the Dictionary, and containing often Webster's rather angry championship.

" Whittle, *v. t.* To pare, or cut off the

surface of a thing with a small knife. Some persons have a habit of *whittling*, and are rarely seen without a penknife in their hands for that purpose. [*This is, I believe, the only use of this word in New England.*]

"Tackle, *v. t.* To harness; as to tackle a horse into a gig, sleigh, coach, or wagon. [*A legitimate and common use of the word in America.*] 2. To seize; to lay hold of; as, a wrestler tackles his antagonist. This is a common popular use of the word in New England, though not elegant. But it retains the primitive idea, to put on, to fall or throw on." The former of these definitions is followed in the latest Webster by the brief parentheses [Prov. Eng. Colloq. U. S.].

"Roiling, *ppr.* Rendering turbid; or exciting the passion of anger. [NOTE: This word is as legitimate as any in the language.]

"Memorialist, *n.* One who writes a memorial. *Spectator.* 2. One who presents a memorial to a legislative or other body, or to a person. *U. States.*

"Emporium. A place of merchandize; a town or city of trade; particularly, a city or town of extensive commerce, or in which an extensive commerce centers, or to which sellers and buyers resort from different countries : such are London, Amsterdam, and Hamburg. New York will be an emporium.

" Emptyings, *n.* The lees of beer, cider, etc.

" Fall, *n.* The fall of the leaf ; the season when leaves fall from trees ; the autumn.

" Avails, *n.*, *plu.* Profits or proceeds. It is used in New England for the proceeds of goods sold, or for rents, issues, or profits.

" Ball, *n.* An entertainment of dancing ; originally and peculiarly at the invitation and expense of an individual ; but the word is used in America for a dance at the expense of the attendant.

" Beadle. An officer in a university whose chief business is to walk with a mace, before the masters, in a public procession ; or, as in America, before the president, trustees, faculty, and students of a college in a procession, at public commencements.

" Commemoration, *n.* The act of calling to remembrance, by some solemnity; the act of honoring the memory of some person or event, by solemn celebration. The feast of shells at Plymouth, in Massachusetts, is an annual commemoration of the first landing of our ancestors in 1620.

" Calculate, *v. i.* To make a computation ; as, we calculate better for ourselves than for others. In *popular use*, this word is often equivalent to *intend* or *purpose*, that is, to make arrangements and form a plan ; as, a man *calculates* to go a journey. This use of the word springs from the practice of *computing* or *estimating* the various circumstances which concur to influence the mind in forming its determinations.

" Shaver, *n.* A boy or young man. This word is still in common use in New England. It must be numbered among our original words.

" Span, *n.* A *span of horses* consists of two of nearly the same color, and otherwise nearly alike, which are usually harnessed side by side. The word signifies properly the same as *yoke*, when applied to horned cattle, from buckling or fastening together. But in America, *span* always implies resemblance in color at least; being an object of ambition with gentlemen and with teamsters to unite two horses abreast that are alike.

" Likely, *a.* Such as may be liked ; pleasing ; as a *likely* man or woman. [This use of *likely* is not obsolete as Johnson affirms, nor is it vulgar. But the English and their descendants in America differ in the application. The English apply the word to external appearance ; and with them *likely* is equivalent to *handsome, well-formed*, as a *likely* man, a *likely* horse. In America the word is usually applied to the endowments of the mind, or to pleasing accomplishments. With us a *likely* man is a man of good character and talents, or of good dispositions or accomplishments, that render him pleasing or respectable.]

" Clever, *a.* In *New England,* good-natured, possessing an agreeable mind or disposition. In *Great Britain* this word is applied to the body or its movements, in its literal sense ; in *America* it is applied chiefly to the mind, temper, disposition. In Great Britain *a clever man* is a dextrous man, one who performs an act with skill or address. In New England *a clever man* is a man of a pleasing, obliging disposition and amiable manners, but often implying a moderate share of talents.

" Raise, *v. t.* To cause to grow; to procure to be produced, bred or propagated; as, to raise wheat, barley, hops, etc.; to *raise* horses, oxen, or sheep. *New England.* [The English now use *grow* in regard to crops; as, to *grow* wheat. This verb intransitive has never been used in New England in a transitive sense, until recently some persons have adopted it from the English books. We always use *raise*, but in New England it is never applied to the breeding of the human race, as it is in the Southern States.]

" Realize, *v. t.* To bring into actual existence and possession; to render tangible or effective. He never *realized* much profit from his trade or speculation.

" Locate, *v. t.*, 2. To select, survey, and settle the bounds of a particular tract of land; or to designate a portion of land by limits; as, to *locate* a tract of a hundred acres in a particular township. *U. States.* 3. To designate and determine the place of; as, a committee was appointed to *locate* a church or a court-house. *N. England.*

" Rail, *n.*, 1. A cross beam fixed at the ends in two upright posts. *Moxon.* [In New England this is never called a *beam;* pieces of timber of the proper size for rails are called *scantling.*] 2. In the *United States* a piece of timber cleft, hewed, or sawed, rough or smooth, inserted in upright posts for fencing. The common *rails* among farmers are rough, being used as they are split from the chestnut or other trees. The *rails* used in fences of boards or pickets round gentlemen's houses and gardens are usually sawed scantling, and often dressed with the plane. 4. A series of posts connected with cross beams, by which a place is inclosed. *Johnson.* In New England we never call this series a *rail*, but by the general term *railing.* In a picket fence, the pales or pickets rise above the rails; in a ballustrade, or fence resembling it, the ballusters usually terminate in the rails.

" Tallow, *n.* A sort of animal fat, particularly that which is obtained from animals of the sheep and ox kinds. . . . The fat of swine we never call *tallow,* but *lard* or *suet.* I see in English books, mention is

made of the tallow of hogs, but in America
I never heard the word thus applied.

" Prairy, *n.* [Fr. *prairie.*] An extensive
tract of land, mostly level, destitute of trees,
and covered with tall, coarse grass. These
prairies are numerous in the United States,
west of the Alleghany Mountains, especially between the Ohio, Mississippi, and
the great lakes.

" Widen, *v. t.* To make wide or wider ;
to extend in breadth ; as, to *widen* a field ;
to *widen* a breach. [Note. In America,
females say, to *widen* a stocking.]

" Window, *n.* An opening in the wall
of a building for the admission of light, and
of air when necessary. This opening has a
frame on the sides, in which are set mov-
able sashes, containing panes of glass. In
the U. States the sashes are made to rise
and fall, for the admission or exclusion
of air. In France *windows* are shut with
frames or sashes that open and shut verti-
cally, like the leaves of a folding door.

" Chore, *n.* [Eng. *char.*] In America this
word denotes small work of a domestic kind,
as distinguished from the principal work of
the day. It is generally used in the plural,

chores, which includes the daily or occasional business of feeding cattle and other animals, preparing fuel, sweeping the house, cleaning furniture, etc. (See char.) "

From these examples one may gather some notion of Webster's method of treating words which were either exclusively American, or had undergone some change in meaning and use. He regards them all not as departures from the English standard of the day, but diversities from an older use, like the English current forms, and it was no disgrace in his eyes for a word to be an Americanism, nor did it require apology or defense of any kind. There are indeed many words not to be found in Johnson, of American origin, or at least of American adoption, which he enters silently with the belief that they have quite as fair a claim to a place in his Dictionary as if they had been used by Dryden or Addison. I have already quoted the passage in his preface relating to the illustrative quotations; the promise made by Webster is faithfully kept, and the diligent reader may garner many of the brief thoughts of Mason, Smith,

Barlow, and other American writers whose
light has now faded.

By all these means, by a certain contempt
of Great Britain, by constant reference to
American usage, by citations from American authors, Webster made the title to his
Dictionary good in every part of it, while
by the exercise of individual caprice and of
a personal authority, which had grown out
of his long-continued and solitary labor,
he attached his own name to it. Both
names remain. The existing Dictionary is
"An American Dictionary of the English
Language," and bears indubitable evidence
of its application to American use, but it is
no longer the organ of an over-zealous patriotism. It bears Noah Webster's name on the
title-page, but the work has been revised,
not out of all likeness to its original form,
but with a fullness and precision which, being impossible to any one man, required the
coöperation of a company of scholars. His
original Preface to the edition of 1828 has
been preserved as a memento of his attitude
in the presence of his great work, but his
Introduction and Advertisement and Grammar of the English Language have been

swept away, and their place supplied by
the maturer and more scholarly work of
Webster's successors.

It has been said by some nice critic, anxious to be just before he was generous, that
the book commonly known as Webster's
Dictionary, sometimes, with a ponderous fa-
miliarity, as The Unabridged, should more
properly be called The Webster Dictionary,
as indicating the fact that the original private enterprise had, as it were, been trans-
formed into a joint stock company, which
might, out of courtesy, take the name of
the once founder but now merely honorary
member of the literary firm engaged in the
manufacture and arrangement of words.
Indeed, the name Webster has been associated with such a vast number of dictionaries of all sizes and weights, that it has
become to many a most impersonal term,
and we may almost expect in a few generations to find the word " Webster " defined
in some revised edition of the Unabridged
as the colloquial word for a Dictionary.
The bright-eyed, bird-like looking gentleman who faces the title-page of his Dictionary may be undergoing some metempsycho-
sis, but the student of American literature

will at any time have little difficulty in res-
cuing his personality from unseemly trans-
migration, and, by the aid of historical
glasses, may discover that the Dictionary
maker, far from being either the arid, blood-
less being which his work supposes, or
the reckless disturber of philological peace
which his enemies aver, was an exceedingly
vigilant, determined American schoolmaster,
who had enormous faith in his country, and
an uncommon self-reliance, by which he
undertook single-handed a task which, once
done, prepared the way for lexigraphical
work far more thorough and satisfactory
than could have been possible without his
pioneer labor. Not only have the successive Dictionaries which bear his name resulted from his labor, but it is not unfair to
refer the other great lexicon begun and carried out by one of his early assistants to the
impetus which he gave. Indeed, the commercial success of the great American Dictionary may reasonably have been taken as
a ground of confidence for the production of
the corresponding works of an encyclopædic and dictionary character which attest
the enterprise of American publishers and
the thoroughness of American scholars.

CHAPTER VIII.

CONCLUSION.

THE publication of "An American Dictionary" in 1828 was followed by increased activity on Dr. Webster's part. He was more than ever ambitious to secure a standard, especially in orthography, and he began the arrangement of his various text-books in a series which should constitute an imposing phalanx, each supporting its neighbor. The work of preparation, revision, and publication occupied the rest of his life. The quarto Dictionary in two volumes cost twenty dollars. He provided soon an abridgment in octavo, and a "Dictionary for Schools, the Counting-House, and for Families in Moderate Circumstances;" he was constantly revising his most lucrative book, the "Elementary Spelling-Book," and he issued new editions of his "History of the United States," his "Teacher," a supplement to the "Elementary," his "Improved Grammar,"

and he prepared a "Manual of Useful Studies." All of these books had friends and
enemies, and one of the most energetic of
the latter, Lyman Cobb, published "a Critical Review of the Orthography of Dr. Webster's Series of Books for Systematick Instruction in the English Language," which,
in spite of some injustice and much quib-
bling, is a most searching and exhaustive
commentary on Webster's weaknesses. The
contest over Webster's Dictionary, however,
did not assume great proportions until after
the publication of Worcester's Dictionary,
which afforded Webster's opponents a flag
about which they could rally. The war of
the dictionaries occurred after Webster's
death, and it is not within the province of
this sketch to enter upon that military campaign. Within Webster's own life-time a
revision of the Dictionary appeared in 1840–
1841, and he was at work upon a further
revision when he died in 1843.

Our study of Webster has easily led us
away from Webster's personal history, except so far as this has illustrated social,
literary, and historical movements. There
are still living those who, as young men,

were associated with him in New Haven, and these with his grandchildren, as well as his only surviving daughter, bear a memory of his person entirely distinct from its public reputation. The resolute old man, working at his lexicography to the last moment, was for them also the tender-hearted head of a family, coming out from his study to hear the music he loved so well, joining in the home life, making affectionate pilgrimages to the old homestead in West Hartford, and putting in a plea there for the preservation of the old fruit trees and vines which dated from his childhood. He was a sturdy, upright man, with the courtesy of an old Federalist, and his figure was a familiar one in the streets of New Haven. It was there that he died, May 28, 1843, in the eighty-fifth year of his age, surrounded by his family, and cheerful with the sense of a full life and of Christian trust and expectation.

Noah Webster's name abides, connected with the great work which he initiated, and the monument will keep his name imperishable. It never can be an uninteresting study to the people how the man, whose

name is a household word, wrought and
achieved; the solid expression of character,
which I have tried to outline, is worthy of
a fuller, more thorough treatment; and it
is to be hoped that the sturdy life of more
than three score years and ten, which he
lived, with its dreams, its discoveries, its
ventures, its toil, and its honest achieve-
ments. may some day be told with all the
minuteness which records, researches, and
reminiscences will permit. Yet I do not
believe the fullest account of Webster would
disclose any important traits not discovered
by the exhibition of such of his writings and
labors as we have included in this survey.
There was nothing concealed in his nature.
His vanity made him open, and his strong
self-reliance gave him a boldness of expression which makes it possible for any student
to measure his aims.

The chief discovery yet to be made of
Webster, if any is possible, lies in the direction of history. I do not suppose that if
the entire correspondence of Webster with
his contemporaries could be produced, we
should find him any more potent as a public man than we have seen him to be; but a

more thorough comprehension of the forces at work in the organization of national life may yet enable us to see with greater distinctness the degree of Webster's power and function. The last result of historical study is the determination of national genius, and for that time and the slow evolution of national character are requisite. I am sure that the dignity of Webster's position in our history is more intelligible to-day than it was in his own time. I am confident that the twentieth century will give him a juster meed than we are giving him to-day.

It was at once his fortune and his misfortune to pass his life contemporaneously with the birth and adolescence of a great nation, and to feel the passion of the hour. There is unquestionably a parochial sort of nationality which it is easy to satirize. No one could well set it out in stronger light than Webster himself in those passages in the preface to his Dictionary which I have already quoted. He is judiciously silent concerning the American poets of his time, being careful, even, — most unkindest cut ! — not to commit himself to the support of Joel

Barlow's heroic verse; but he produces a
list of American prosaists, whom he places
back to back with their English fellows. He
has a proper sense of the importance of language to a nation, and appears to be per-
plexed by the implied question : If Englishmen and Americans speak the same language, how in the world are we to tell them
apart and keep them apart? Then again,
since there has been a revolution resulting
in governmental independence, what stands
in the way of a complete independence, so
that the spick and span new nation may go
to the language tailors and be dressed in a
new suit of parts of speech? " Let us seize
the present moment," he cries, " and establish a national language as well as a national government." Never was there such
a chance, he thinks, for clearing away the
rubbish which has accumulated for generations in our clumsy, inelegant language.
Hand him the Bible which people have
foolishly regarded as a great conservator of
the English tongue, and he will give you a
new edition "purified from the numerous
errors." Knock off the useless appendages
to words which serve only to muffle simple

sounds. Innocent iconoclast, with his school-master ferrule !

It is worth our while to make serious answer to these serious propositions, since the true aspect of native literature may thus be disclosed. The Revolution, which so filled Webster's eyes, was unquestionably a great historic event by reason of its connection with the formal institution of a new nation; but the roots of our national life were not then planted. They run back to the first settlements and the first charters and agreements ; nor is the genesis of the nation to be found there ; sharp as are the beginnings of our history on this continent, no student could content himself with a conception of our national life which took into account only the events and conditions determined by the people and the soil of America. Even in actual relations between America and Europe there never has been a time when the Atlantic has not had an ebbing as well as a flowing tide, and the instinct which now sends us to the Old World on passionate pilgrimages is a constituent part of our national life, and not an unfilial sentiment. In the minds of Webster and many others,

England was an unnatural parent, and the
spirit of anger, together with an elation at
success in the severing of governmental ties,
made them impatient of even a spiritual
connection. But the Revolution was an outward, visible sign of an organic growth
which it accelerated, but did not produce ;
and the patriotic outcries of the generation
were incoherent expressions of a profounder
life which had been growing, scarcely
heeded, until wakened by this event. The
centripetal force of nationality was at work,
and it is possible now, even from our near
station, to discover the conjunction of outward circumstance and inward consciousness which marks nationality as an established fact. It was a weak conception of
nationality which was bounded by Webster's definition ; but his belief in his country and his energetic action were, in real-
ity, constantly overpassing that conception.
In spite of the disposition to regard a written constitution as the bottom fact, there
was the real, substantial, organic nation, and
that saved the paper nation from erasure, —
a fate which easily overtakes South American republics. A nation which could im-

mediately be placed in the world's museum, duly ticketed and catalogued, with its distinct manners, dress, language, and literature, — this was a conception which resulted logically from theories which held the nation itself to be the creation of popular will or historic accident; but a nation slowly struggling against untoward outward circumstance and inward dissension, collecting by degrees its constituent members, forming and reforming, plunging with rude strength down dangerous ways, but nevertheless growing into integral unity, — this has been the historical result of the living forces which were immanent in the country when the nation was formally instituted.

Now there never has been a time from Webster's day to this when Americans have not believed and asserted that nationality consisted mainly in independence, and waxed impatient not merely of foreign control and influence, but even of hereditary influence : the temper which calls for American characteristics in art and literature is often scarcely less hostile to the past of American history than to the present of European civilization. It is a restless, uneasy

spirit, goaded by self-consciousness. It finds
in nature an aid and abettor; it grows angry at the disproportionate place which the
Cephissus, the Arno, the Seine, the Rhine,
and the Thames hold on the map of the
world's passion. We are all acquainted
with the typical American who added to his
name in the hotel book on the shores of
Lake Como, "What pygmy puddles these
are to the inland seas of tremendous and
eternal America!" But these are coarser,
more palpable signs of that uneasy consciousness which frets at a continued dependence on European culture.

There is no doubt that Webster was right
when he set himself the task of Americaniz-
ing the English language by a recourse to the
Spelling-Book. He succeeded very largely
in determining the form of words; but he
did more than this, while he failed in the
ambitious and preposterous task which he
set himself. He did more; by his shrewdness and his ready perception of the popular need he made elementary education possible at once, and furnished the American
people with a key which moved easily in
the lock; he failed where he sought the

most, because language is not a toy or a patent machine, which can be broken, thrown
aside at will, and replaced with a better
tool, ready-made from the lexicographer's
shop. He had no conception of the enormous weight of the English language and
literature, when he undertook to shovel it
out of the path of American civilization.
The stars in their courses fought against
him. It is so still. We cannot dispense
with European culture, because we refuse
to separate ourselves from the mighty past,
which has settled there in forms of human
life unrepresented among us. We cannot
step out of the world's current, though it
looks sluggish beside our rushing stream,
because there is a spiritual demand in us
which cries louder than the thin voice of a
self-conscious national life. This demand
is profoundly at one with the deeper, holier
sense of national being which does not strut
upon the world's stage. The humility of a
great nation is in its reverence for its own
past, and, since that is incomplete, in its ad-
miration for whatever is noble and worthy
in other nations. It is out of this reverence
and humility and this self-respect that great

works in literature and art grow, and not
out of the overweening sensitiveness which
makes one's nationality but a petty jealousy
of other people.

It is possible for us thus to discriminate
between a nationality which is a mere post-
ure and that which is a plain expression of
positive organic life. When we measure
the force of the latter we are compelled to
a finer analysis, and its illustrations are to
be sought in subtler manifestations. Webster well exemplifies, by the very rudeness
of his mind, phases of Americanism which
may be traced in more delicate lines elsewhere. There can be no doubt that self-
reliance, which was both the cause and the
effect of local self-government long practiced, has been a powerful factor in American life; that an indifference to the past
has often been only the obverse of an elastic
hope, a consciousness of destiny; that a fear-
lessness and a spirit of adventure have been
invited by the large promises held out by
nature; that an expansiveness of mind, and
an alertness and facility in intellectual device, have been encouraged by the flexile
condition of American society. All things

have seemed possible to the ardent American, and each has secretly said to himself : —

"I . . . had resolved to be
The maker of my destiny."

These elements of character have entered into literature, the exponent of character; and Webster, with his self-reliance, his indifference to the past, his consciousness of destiny, his courage and resolution and quick fitting into his country's work, stands easily as the first aggressive American in our literature. In him we see roughly marked what future critics will discern of men more readily assigned a place in universal literature. The Americanism of Hawthorne, for example, differs from that of Webster in quality rather than in essence. They were both content with America and New England. Hawthorne, with his shrug at old buildings and his wish that all over two hundred years of age should be burnt down, was repeating Webster's contempt of the musty halls of collegiate Cambridge ; and Hawthorne, Yankeeizing the Greek myths, and finding all Rome but the background for his Puritan maiden, was asserting that

19

new discovery of Europe by America which
has ever since been going on, and was illustrated by Webster's excursions in language
to bring back English variations from American usage.

The ease with which Webster walked
about the Jericho of English lexicography,
blowing his trumpet of destruction, was an
American ease, born of a sense that America was a continent and not a province. He
transferred the capital of literature from
London to Boston, or New York, or Hartford, — he was indifferent so long as it was
in the United States. He thought Washington as good an authority on spelling as
Dr. Johnson, and much better than King
George. He took the Bible as a book to
be used, not as a piece of antiquity to be
sheltered in a museum, and with an American practicality set about making it more
serviceable in his own way. He foresaw
the vast crowds of American children; he
knew that the integrity of the country was
conditioned on the intelligibility of their
votes, and he turned his back on England
less with indifference to her than with an
absorption in his own country. He made a

Speller which has sown votes and muskets; he made alone a Dictionary, which has grown, under the impulse he gave it, into a national encyclopædia, possessing an irresistible momentum. Indeed, is not the very existence of that book in its current form a witness to the same Americanism which Webster displayed, only now in a firmer, finer, and more complex form?

In the high walks of scholarship, where nationality would seem to be effaced, we have had very recently a capital illustration of the inevitable tendency of national traits to seek expression. The Appendix to the "Revised Version of the New Testament" contains the variations proposed by the American company from the text as otherwise determined. There were in the English company men of radical temperament and of conservative; there were in the American company like distinctions; nevertheless the final separation between the two companies is largely on this line, and one can easily see how much sympathy, Webster, for example, would have expressed with the position which the American company took, a position not of dissent but of independent assertion.

The separation between England and America which was so effectual in Webster's conception, and thus determined much of his thought, was really incipient and not complete. The two countries are more widely separate to-day than they were then, while the outward signs of separation are in many ways less conspicuous. The forces of national life have been diverging, and the resultant in character and literature is more sure and ineffaceable.

It should be observed that the individualism which characterizes American life was more marked in the first years of the republic than it is now. After we have reasoned away all we will of a revolutionary cataclysmal element in the separation of the United States from the British Empire, there still remains a sharp determination of individual life, historically evident, and very influential in the formation of national character. In the earliest years the centripetal force for union was barely superior to the centrifugal force for state independence; but the political thought which justified state sovereignty had its logical issue in an isolated individuality. Common sense and prudence, to be sure, are always defeating logic; but the logical conception helps us to understand tendencies, and it is not difficult to see that the word independence, which was on every one's lips at the close of the last century, was not the sign of a political thought only, but expressed the habit of mind with which persons everywhere regarded life in its varied relations. The breaking up of old political connections not only unsettled the social fabric, it affected necessarily all the relations which the person held to society; and it was only as a profounder political unity disclosed itself in the nation that each man put forth more confidently his hand to his fellow. The historian of the Union will not fail to observe how with the growth of that Union there began to spring up societies and corporations of every kind, the interdependence of the States extending itself to the interdependence of all interests involved in the State, and the whole fabric of society feeling its web and woof grow firmer and denser.

The career of Webster illustrates this truth. He worked alone, and his solitariness was not wholly due to his idiosyncrasies. It was in part the penalty paid by a student of the time. The resolution and self-reliance of an American were his, and so was the individuality. That such enterprises are not now conducted single-handed is owing not to a lack of courage but to the greater complexity of life, the more constant sense of interdependence, the existence of greater solidarity in intellectual pursuits. Webster was unable to believe that a company of scholars could ever be formed who should carry forward a revision of the Bible, and therefore he made the attempt himself. Individual criticism has been abundant ever since, but no one, however learned or popular, has ever been able to impress his work upon the community. The most carefully organized body of scholars submits the results of its ten years' conference to the votes of the world. The history of Webster's Dictionary is parallel with the growth of national life out of individualism.

INDEX.

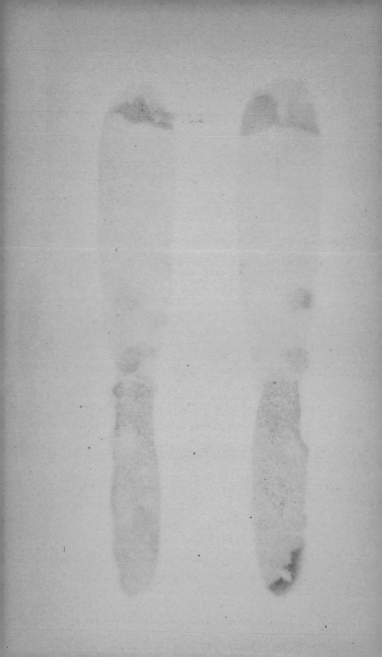